THE 365 DAY LEADER

Recalibrate Your Calling Every Day

The 365 Day Leader: Recalibrate Your Calling Every Day
© 2024 by Dick Daniels

All rights reserved under International Copyright Law.
Contents and/or cover may not be reproduced
in whole or in part in any form without the express
written consent of the publisher.

Hardcover ISBN: 979-8-9908193-0-6
Paperback ISBN: 979-8-9908193-1-3
ePub ISBN: 979-8-9908193-2-0

Leadership Development Group

Cover and interior design:
The Brand Office

A WORD FROM MARSHALL GOLDSMITH

"*The 365 Day Leader* is a treasure trove for any leader seeking daily motivation and inspiration to navigate the complexities of modern businesses and teams. Each quote is a nugget of wisdom, encouraging reflection and inspiring action to foster leadership that is not only effective, but also filled with integrity and purpose. Dr. Daniels' work is a testament to the power of leadership transformation — one day at a time."

DR. MARSHALL GOLDSMITH is the Thinkers50 #1 Executive Coach and New York Times bestselling author of *The Earned Life*, *Triggers*, and *What Got You Here Won't Get You There*

ABOUT THE BOOK

The 365 Day Leader is the newest addition in the Leadership Development Group library. It offers a daily resource to recalibrate your leadership calling every day of the year. It includes a reference guide to direct the reader to specific leadership topics when looking for that sixty-second insight into a question being asked at a particular leadership intersection. *The 365 Day Leader* will not only inspire the supervisor, manager, or leader at any level in every company, but it will also provide a suggested plan for how to use the quote format for team discussions and action planning. This comprehensive volume is the best of the Leadership Development Group's thinking about how to enhance effectiveness and efficiency in leaders and the teams they lead.

ALSO BY THE AUTHOR

Leadership Briefs: Shaping Organizational Culture to Stretch Leadership Capacity

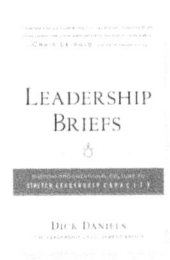

A challenge for senior leadership in any company is to shape an organizational culture that accelerates the development of seasoned and emerging leaders. Practical insights into the development structures and systems needed to equip supervisors, managers, and leaders for readiness to lead at higher levels of organizational complexity. Nationally awarded: Midwest Book Awards and Reader Views Reviewers Choice Award.

Leadership Core: Character, Competence, Capacity

When leaders develop character, alongside developing leadership competence, it enhances their overall leadership capacity. Who you are in your core values and how well you do what you do determine how high you can lead. Two character multipliers, three competence multipliers, and two capacity multipliers provide the framework for this leadership development resource. Nationally awarded: Nautilus Book Award and Reader Views Reviewers Choice Award.

Hardwiring New Leadership Habits: Does Development Develop?

Follow the fictional story of the CEO of Global Organization Resources, Inc. and her executive team during their three-day, strategic offsite meeting. Hardwiring provides a measured discussion guide for executive teams in any organization as they evaluate their current and future commitment to create a development culture that invests in the productive potential of every employee. Nationally awarded: Readers' Favorite Book Award.

Table of Contents

PREFACE 11

INTRODUCTION 13

JANUARY 17

FEBRUARY 53

MARCH 85

APRIL 121

MAY 155

JUNE 191

JULY 225

AUGUST 261

SEPTEMBER 297

OCTOBER 331

NOVEMBER 367

DECEMBER 401

AFTERWORD 436

THE 365 DAY LEADER DEBRIEF 439

ACKNOWLEDGEMENTS 441

ABOUT THE AUTHOR 443

TOPIC REFERENCE GUIDE 445

LEAD UNOFFENDED 449

PREFACE

There are two kinds of leaders:

1) Life-long, learning leaders who salivate over a new leadership book. This tribe affirms: "I can still improve as a leader."

2) Leaders who don't read anymore. They believe the lie that leadership enrichment is not worth the investment.

If you're still reading this preface (and who reads the preface anyway?)... you're clearly a life-long, learning leader. Dick Daniels' insights and wisdom are book-of-the-year worthy.

Every time Dick wordcrafts a leadership lesson—I'm stunned. Ask me how to build a healthy culture, and I can give you a few ideas and a couple books to read. But then I read his first book, *Leadership Briefs*, where Dick delivers eight core elements and seven specific steps. (It's off-the-chart savvy!)

My first thought when reading his second book, *Leadership Core*, was: "I could have used this book years ago—and saved myself and my team members from unnecessary leadership pain." (Hint: The chapter on delegation is worth the price of the book!)

In his third book, *Hardwiring New Leadership Habits*, Daniels shocks us with this: "People lie more on Monday and Friday than on Tuesday, Wednesday, or Thursday." (Note: I wrote this on a Wednesday!) Dick shares five scenarios when your staff might be tempted to lie. (I did not know this!)

So, why do we need 365 daily nudges on leadership? The late Zig Ziglar wrote, "People often say that motivation doesn't last. Well, neither does bathing—that's why we recommend it daily." I'm loving my daily dose of Dick Daniels.

Thanks for writing *The 365 Day Leader*!

– JOHN PEARSON, Management Consultant and Author,
Mastering the Management Buckets, *Mastering 100 Must-Read Books*,
and *Mastering Mistake-Making*

INTRODUCTION

Recalibrate Your Calling

The leadership ideas, insights, and best practices included in *The 365 Day Leader* represent the best thinking of The Leadership Development Group and will enhance the capacity of any supervisor, manager, or leader. Each original quote contributes to the life-long learning agenda of growing leaders who are committed to greater effectiveness and efficiency by hardwiring new leadership habits. Development is incremental in each iteration of professional career planning when learning and personal action is the focus.

Each quote is a snapshot of what exemplary leaders consistently do. The uniqueness of this book is that we answer the "So what?" question. The ideas included are at points inspirational and at other points challenging. So, what do you do as the reader beyond being inspired or challenged? Learning without application is merely an academic exercise that adds one more book to your already overloaded bookshelf.

The "How To" plan answers the "So what?" question. The scenario below reflects your use of *The 365 Day Leader* with a team of your direct reports who meet weekly. If you meet on a different rhythm, then adjust your use of the six "How To" steps. Allow ten to twelve minutes for this application exercise. It can be done that efficiently!

1. Review the seven quotes from the previous week. This assumes that each team member has the list of quotes for that week.

2. Vote on the top quote that has the greatest relevance for your organization at this point in time. Let everyone rank their top three quotes and calculate the top selection out of all votes cast. This could even be completed prior to your meeting.

3. Discuss the top quote. How do people understand what it means for your company and why is it relevant for today?

INTRODUCTION

4. Then answer these two action planning questions: "If we took this statement to heart, what would we have to do differently? What are the implications inherent in this quote?" List all the ideas on a white board or on a screen document for viewing.

5. Go around the group, letting each direct report select one action idea for personal application. Ask each one to "behavioralize" their application. What does their action step look like in one specific aspect of their own leadership behavior with those they lead and in their relationships with peers and senior leadership? This is not new work. It's even not more work. It is doing the work they are already doing, but just a little differently. Keep it simple. Don't let the "thinkers" overcomplicate the simplicity of the process even though the outcome can be quite profound.

6. As the senior leader of this team, check in with each direct report once during the week to ask how it's going. This is not a formal one on one but an informal huddle conversation that only takes a minute or two. This accountability contributes to incremental change in building new habits. That's when new leadership habits are hardwired. What we hold people accountable for is what they tend to do.

My advice as the author is that this six-step "How To" plan is a tool. Use the tool; don't be used by the tool. Knowing and understanding the relevant ideas included in *The 365 Day Leader* never changes anything. Application is the transformer. Do something with what you now know and now understand more deeply. The value in the format of this book is the incremental adventure of recalibrating your calling on a daily basis.

Learning and Growing with You!

Dr. D ...

DICK DANIELS
Certified Master Coach for Successful Executives
Founder and President, The Leadership Development Group

www.theLDG.org ≈ *Dd@theLDG.org*

MONTH 01

JANUARY

MONTH

The 365 Day Pillars

"Leadership Development Foundations" shape the culture of an organization that values the development of every team member. That value leads to an investment that equips every supervisor, manager, and leader for greater productivity in their current role or in a role with greater complexity and responsibility.

"Leadership Development Pathways" provide clarity for each employee of how to move forward in their professional development. A customized plan identifies needed learning and the expectation of application with measurable goals and related action planning. Great organizations move high potential team members from a larger talent pool into a leadership development pipeline.

"Leadership Development Hardwiring" is the means of sustaining new leadership habits. Coaching, stakeholder feedback, and personal reflection lead to incremental change. Since leadership is a learned competency, leaders never stop learning and refining their leadership practice. It's not new work or more work, but learning to do the work you are already doing ... but differently.

JANUARY

THE HOW TO OF RECALIBRATING YOUR LEADERSHIP CALLING

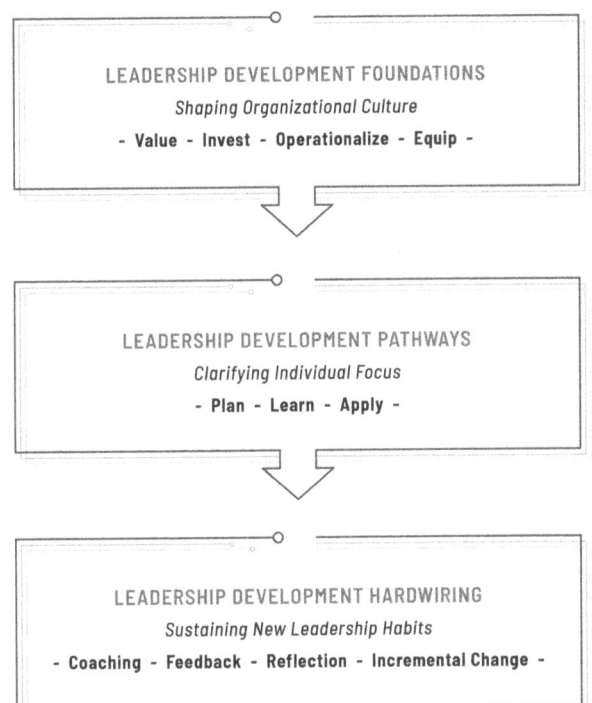

LEADERSHIP DEVELOPMENT FOUNDATIONS
Shaping Organizational Culture
- Value - Invest - Operationalize - Equip -

LEADERSHIP DEVELOPMENT PATHWAYS
Clarifying Individual Focus
- Plan - Learn - Apply -

LEADERSHIP DEVELOPMENT HARDWIRING
Sustaining New Leadership Habits
- Coaching - Feedback - Reflection - Incremental Change -

DAY 1

What Does Your Company Value?

When organizations only value the bottom line, three things result:

1. Leadership Competence is rewarded.
2. Leadership Character is assumed.
3. Leadership Capacity is never fully realized.

Character & Competence

Character **minus** Competence = I like you, but I don't respect you.

Competency **minus** Character = I respect you, but I don't like you.

Have You Ever Had a Coach?

The leadership delusion is to assume everyone needs a coach except you.

The Personal and Interpersonal Sides of Character

Integrity is the perception others have of you by observing the consistency of your attitudes, words and behavior.

Respect is the perception you have of others as expressed in your attitudes, words, and behaviors about people who may not be like you or may not like you.

Succeeding in Succession Planning

Succession planning is the process to identify critical positions in your company while designing pathways with realistic timelines for internal or external candidates to be considered for those positions. A rule of thumb: Successions will take twice as long as you assume.

JANUARY

Personal Drive Is the Distinguisher

Personal Drive is the inner motivation that makes a leader pay the price to succeed. Some have it. Some never will.

Ethics at Play

Ethical leadership adheres to foundational principles and values that establish the organizational culture of how teams agree to work together. Integrity, respect, honesty, trust, fairness, and transparency to name a few.

Organizational Health

When your company is healthy, leaders are more effective. When leaders are healthy, teams are more effective.

Health indicators include: clarity of vision, realistic strategy, employee satisfaction, and a values-driven culture.

Leadership Requirements

Leadership competence is the effectiveness and efficiency in using the skills and resources required for your role

The Core Triad

Character is the core pathway to positive influence.

Competence is the core pathway to effective action.

Capacity is the core pathway to leadership potential.

What Is Your Capacity to Lead?

Character reflects the consistency of who you are publicly and privately.

Competence addresses the effectiveness and efficiency in using the skills required for your role.

Capacity speaks to your ability and readiness to lead at higher levels of organizational complexity.

DAY 12

Productive Potential

Your company's value of professional development determines its ability to achieve today's productive potential.

Your individual investment in hardwiring new leadership habits determines your capacity to lead at higher levels of organizational complexity.

DAY 13

What It Takes to Become a Developmental Culture?

Developmental organizations make developmental teams possible. Developmental teams make developing individuals possible. When all three intersect and work together toward the same vision, mission, and values, then the engagement and productivity of every team member increases.

The organization is critical.

The Team is essential.

The individual is nonnegotiable.

Yes or No

Leadership capacity increases when leaders say "Yes" to the right things and "No" to the wrong things. When did you last say "No?" What is something you keep procrastinating on that you need to say "Yes" to?

Museum Terminology

A "Curator" is defined as the keeper or custodian of a museum or other collections. Leaders are "Curators" of organizational culture which is the collection of the company's vision, mission, values, and strategy.

Day 16

Valuing Development

The organization's cultural value of professional development flows from the organization to the individual (trickle down) and from the individual through the team to the organization (trickle up). That is the dynamic nature of developmental cultures.

Ethics Made Easy

Wrong is never right even if everyone does it.

Right is never wrong even if no one does it.

DAY 18

There Is Bias in Judging a Leader by the Worst Decision They Ever Made

Has it been done to you?

Have you done it to others?

The Consistency of Your Attitudes, Words, and Actions

Attitudes – The perceived expression you bring into situations regarding people and circumstances.

Words – The oral expression of your attitudes demonstrated verbally and non-verbally.

Actions – The behavioral expression of your attitudes and words.

There is no trust, respect, or influence without consistency.

DAY 20

The Five Questions to Keep Asking

The Context Question: What did we used to do?

The Reality Question: What are we doing today?

The Change Question: What should we do differently?

The Priority Question: What should we do next?

The Letting-Go Question: What should we stop doing?

Smart leaders regularly ask team members all five questions.

Which question do you rarely, if ever, ask?

Connecting the Leader to the Organization

Leadership development represents an investment in growing supervisors, managers, and leaders at their point of greatest need connected to the organization's greatest opportunities.

DAY 22

The Means and The End

Leadership...

It's always a means to an end...

and never an end in itself.

What Are Your Priorities?

The capacity of a leader increases when they protect their time and their priorities to address the important more than the urgent.

The Three Levels of Leadership Development

Level One – Team members can't achieve professional development without the team leader's encouragement and support.

Level Two – Supervisors, managers, and leaders can't develop team members if the organization doesn't value a developmental culture.

Level Three – Organizations can't live out the value of a development culture unless it invests in the resources needed for development at every level of employment.

The Context of Leading

Leadership behavior must always reflect organizational values.

Leadership competency must always align with strategic outcomes.

Leadership development must always address the behaviors that affect outcomes.

DAY 26

The Question of Values

Organizational values are not just ideas to believe but interpersonal behaviors to model with every team member, vendor, customer, and even every competitor.

DAY 27

The Delegation Dilemma

What could you stop doing?

What should you stop doing?

What will you stop doing?

Handing Off. Delegation is all about developing high potential team members with the readiness to take on responsibilities you should no longer be doing.

Letting Go. Delegation is complete when you not only give the responsibility but also the authority to complete each delegated assignment.

DAY 28

Two Kinds of Leaders

The Urgent Leader rarely has time to delegate under the self-imposed burden of hanging on to tasks that others on their team could be equipped over time to do. These leaders say: "I can do it faster and better, and I don't have time to get someone else up to speed to do this. We are always under pressure to meet new deadlines, and I just have to keep doing these things."

The Important Leader develops direct reports in order to delegate the details of tactical operations and recapture time for the work of strategy. These leaders say: "As the senior leader of this team, it is my responsibility to reserve time to strategically assess our current reality, see around the corner of where we need to be in the future, and determine how to get there."

DAY 29

When Did You Last Say…?

Recognition is a motivator in every team member's performance. It gives a sense of accomplishment. It expresses appreciation for the work each team member contributes. It clarifies how success is defined in the mind of the leader. It is essential in any retention strategy. When is the last time you said, "Thank you" to each direct report. It's not complicated. The mistake is always waiting too long to say it.

DAY 30

Final Interview Questions

The Professional Competence Question: Can they do the job?

The Personal Drive Question: Do they want to do the job?

The Cultural Fit Question: Will we like them while they do the job?

Learning to Apply...
Applying to Grow

... Identify the skills needed in your current role.

... Invest in micro-learning to increase your understanding.

... Incrementally apply specific new skills that lead to new habits.

... Use feedback and reflection to guide your next iteration of development.

MONTH 02

FEBRUARY

MONTH 02

An Organizational Assessment of the Development Value

Ten continuums provide the executive leadership team an honest appraisal of how intentionally and how effectively the organization has operationalized their stated value of offering a development pathway for every team member.

FEBRUARY

An Organizational Diagnosis:

How Valued is Development?

① ② ③ ④ ⑤ ⑥ ⑦ ⑧ ⑨ ⑩

Uncertainty of mission, vision, values	— or —	Clarity of mission, vision, values
No development pathway exists here	— or —	We value and guide in professional development
Employee disengagement	— or —	Employee engagement
Employee dissatisfaction	— or —	Employee satisfaction
Too many people miss expectations	— or —	Most people meet or exceed expectations
Team silos	— or —	Team collaboration
"It's good enough"	— or —	We strive to achieve our org's productive potential
"We've always done it that way"	— or —	We are committed to continual improvement
Leaders are the exception to the rule	— or —	Leaders model the way
"Just hire someone soon"	— or —	We have a leadership pipeline

A Leader's Unfinished Business

Throughout the year, pay attention to any unfinished business with each member of your team. Own your miscues, mistakes, misspoken words, misunderstandings, and misappropriate attitudes, words, or behaviors. Here is how to start: "I'm sorry for..."

DAY 33

"Pihsredael"

Yes, we get "leadership" spelled backwards.
Leading is not about your team making you look good.
Your sole responsibility is to help each of your direct reports be successful in their assignments. How?

... Knowing the uniqueness of each team member.

... Investing in opportunities for continuing development.

... Matching strengths to assignments.

... Defining success with clarity.

... Providing every resource needed for timely completion.

... Supporting just enough as needed.

... Holding accountable to meet benchmarks.

... Recognition for a job well done.

... Celebrating contributions to organizational outcomes.

Some Leaders Are Born. Most Leaders are Made.

... Coaching helps identify the competencies needing further development.

... Micro-learning increases one's understanding in order to apply new ideas.

... New skills lead to incremental change in one's habits of leading.

... Feedback and reflection guide the next iteration of learning and application.

DAY 35

Time for Reflection

… Assessments offer **objective accountability**. Team feedback provides **organizational accountability**. Reflection is the process of **personal accountability**.

… Reflection is your own solitary assignment for self-vulnerability and self-transparency. The concepts of "Sabbath" and "Sanctuary" are a reminder that reflection in our leadership development journey needs a regular time and a consistent place to heighten the value and significance of taking time out for personal review and assessment of one's progress.

DAY 36

The Toxic Team Member

Waiting too long while making well-intended attempts to bring the toxic team member up, brings everyone else down.

Two Laws of Professional Development

Law #1 – Manageable Expectations

Don't take on too much at once.

Law #2 – Change Incrementally

Application of new habits is done in iterations.

FEBRUARY

Leaders & Followers

How well leaders lead ...

Affects ...

How well followers follow.

When both lead and follow well ...

Then becoming a high performing team is possible.

Does Development Develop?

It begins when the organization values and invests in the incremental development of every team member with clarity of the necessary pathway and a picture of what it leads to.

DAY 40

The Hardwiring New Leadership Habits Model

Stage One – Leadership Development Foundations Shape Organizational Culture

When companies value, invest, and create development pathways.

Stage Two – Leadership Development Pathways Clarify Individual Focus

When team members focus new learning on application in order to develop new leadership habits.

Stage Three – Leadership Development Hardwiring Sustains New Leadership Habits

When organizations offer coaching, create feedback systems, allow time for individual reflection, and expect incremental change in each iteration of professional development.

Meeting Overload?

If you are in meetings all day, when do you get your work done? Yes, you bring value to every meeting you attend, but is it time to equip a direct report to be your **Meeting Ambassador** in some of the meetings you currently attend? Use a priority matrix to help sort out the important meetings from the urgent meetings. Give your first meeting away today.

... When you do, you are developing a high-potential direct report to stretch their skill set in new ways.

... When you do, then you recapture time for more strategic aspects of leading.

DAY 42

"A Leader is a Dealer in Hope"

— *Napolean Bonaparte*

| 1 | 2 | 3 | 4 | 5 | 6 | 7 | 8 | 9 | 10 |

HOPELESS — HOPEFUL

Where would your team rate you on the continuum in three areas:

Attitudes – How you reflect hope in your persona.

Words – How you reflect hope in what you say and how you say it.

Behavior – How you reflect hope in how you live.

Building a Culture of Respect, Trust, and Loyalty

The more humility in the leader, the greater the respect, trust, and loyalty.

The less humility in the leader, the less respect, trust, and loyalty.

Humility Defined

Saying less about yourself than you think you deserve and saying less than you think others need to hear.

Know Your Team

If you don't know the uniqueness of each direct report, then you will never understand how to uniquely develop them either.

New Contacts Do Count

Strategic networking within or outside your company not only enhances your business acumen, but these new connections open the door to new opportunities. New opportunities bring stretch experiences that add meaning and fulfillment to life and work.

FEBRUARY

DAY 46

Recognition. Reward. Celebration.

When did you last party with your team?

Recognition – Watch, Notice, Remember, and Tell the Team Member.

Reward – Each team member who exceeds expectations.

Celebration – When your team meets or surpasses goals.

Identity – Who You Think You Are
Reputation – Who Others Think You Are

In leadership, your reputation is more important than your identity. Reputation is the perception of how effectively you lead by those who follow. What might you need to do to change those perceptions?

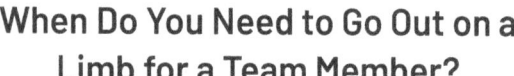

When Do You Need to Go Out on a Limb for a Team Member?

The Professional Side of Leading

When you advocate for training, resources, and support so a team member effectively handles work obstacles and opportunities.

The Personal Side of Leading

When a team member brings the messiness of life to work, and it interferes with productivity.

The Four Sides of Leadership

Leadership is influencing, inspiring, and resourcing your team to:

Side One – Own the strategy.

Side Two – Engage in the daily mission.

Side Three – Live out the organizational values.

Side Four – Understand their contribution to vision achievement.

FEBRUARY

No Joke

It's no joke that leaders are human ...

It's no joke that leaders make mistakes ...

It's no joke that great leaders admit it!

Who's Accountable

If leadership implies getting work done with and through other people, then immediate feedback and consistent accountability are the non-negotiables.

FEBRUARY

Terminating the Underperformer

Procrastinating the tough but necessary decision about the underperforming team member negatively impacts the morale of your organizational culture and, as a result, you diminish the productive potential of the entire team.

Leadership Braggarts

Reality. The further up the hierarchy, the greater your resources to buy more things and go more places. Yes, you've earned it. No apologies needed.

Perception. When you have the need to talk about it all with those down the hierarchy, you are diminishing the life situation of your team members.

Solution. Be mindful of your comments about possessions and travel that others may never have the resources to attain. Rather than talk about your world, find ways to talk about theirs.

FEBRUARY

Leadership as Asking and Telling

Most leaders err on the side of telling more than asking. When you ask, then you are in a position to listen to what a team member is saying without assuming, without interrupting, and without merely thinking about what you might say next.

... Listening is a learned competency.

... Active listening is the ability to restate what someone just said.

... Intentional listening is focused on understanding not agreement.

... Learn to ask more than you tell.

Leadership Words Matter

Tomorrow, you may not remember what you said today, but some of your words may stick with a team member forever.

Leadership Development Consequences

It's so much better to develop your supervisors, managers, and leaders even if they leave, rather than not develop them and they stay.

The Leadership Development Goal

Great leaders are lifelong learners ... and,

Great leaders are lifelong appliers ... who,

Change incrementally in every iteration of development.

Leaders with an Ethical Edge

Relative ethics is self-serving when the end always justifies the means (no matter how mean it is). How about just doing what's right?

DAY 59

The Leadership Guardrail of Workplace Relationships

Emotions are the currency of how team members work together. Your emotional filter is the guardrail in every interpersonal relationship.

… *You're feeling something.*

… That's normal!

… *How, when, where, to whom, and with what level of intensity will you express it?*

… That's emotional intelligence.

Your executive presence as a leader is determined by how smart you are emotionally.

MONTH 03

MARCH

RECALIBRATE YOUR CALLING EVERY DAY

MONTH 03

Comparing Character and Competence

When leadership development addresses both character (Soft Skills) and competence (Hard Skills), it expands one's capacity to lead at higher levels of organizational complexity.

MARCH

Six Distinguishing Characteristics

Leadership Character	Gets at Who You Are	Tied to Organizational Culture	All About Values	Soft Skills of Leadership	Impacts Relationships	Positive Influence
Leadership Competence	Gets at What You Do	Tied to the Bottom Line	All About Strategy	Hard Skills of Leadership	Impacts Results	Effective Action

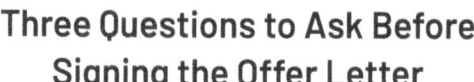

Three Questions to Ask Before Signing the Offer Letter

1. Will I like and respect the people I work with and work for?

2. Can I thrive here by developing my strengths to enhance my productive potential and contribute to the company's strategic outcomes?

3. Do my values align with the organization's values as stated and as practiced in daily business conversations and negotiations.

Listening Questions #1

What do I need to know from you today?

If you could change one thing in our company, what would you change?

What is the best part of your job?

Listening Questions #2

What did you accomplish this week?

What challenges or obstacles did you run into?

What are your goals to achieve next week?

Listening Questions #3

The Obvious Question: Do you need my help?

The Check-In Question: How are you keeping me informed at key decision points?

The Development Question: What skills or resources were needed for this project that we were not aware of at the outset?

Leadership is Contextual

Organizational culture is the context within which leaders develop.

… The healthier the organization, the more effective the leader.

… The healthier the leader, the more effective the organization.

DAY 65

Three Leadership Beliefs

Belief #1 – Leaders are more made than born.

Belief #2 – Leadership is a lifelong incremental process of developmental iterations.

Belief #3 – Organizational needs determine the leadership competency priorities needed for success.

MARCH

DAY 66

Ethical Leadership

Truth always outlives a lie.

DAY 67

Leadership to the Extreme

Arrogant leaders expect perfection in everyone but themselves.

MARCH

Asking, Listening, and Talking

Leaders who don't ask insightful questions end up doing all the talking.

The 11 Laws of Hardwiring New Leadership Habits: Law #1

New leadership habits are more likely to be sustainable when your organization values and invests in the development of supervisors, managers, and leaders at every level.

The 11 Laws of Hardwiring New Leadership Habits: Law #2

New leadership habits are more sustainable when your company creates pathways to development for every supervisor, manager, and leader.

DAY 71

The 11 Laws of Hardwiring New Leadership Habits: Law #3

The organizational culture is developmental at its core.

DAY 72

The 11 Laws of Hardwiring New Leadership Habits: Law #4

Leaders have the personal drive to keep getting better as their lifelong learning always leads to application.

The 11 Laws of Hardwiring New Leadership Habits: Law #5

Incremental change in effectiveness and efficiency is strengthened when leaders commit to leadership development coaching with ongoing feedback from key stakeholders on their team and across the organization.

The 11 Laws of Hardwiring New Leadership Habits: Law #6

Hardwiring new leadership habits occurs when organizational vision, mission, and values include a commitment to develop supervisors, managers, and leaders throughout the company.

The 11 Laws of Hardwiring New Leadership Habits: Law #7

New leadership habits endure when personal and professional development is manageable and incremental.

DAY 76

The 11 Laws of Hardwiring New Leadership Habits: Law #8

The business case for organizational investment in professional development convinces the financial skeptic by collecting and analyzing the relevant data that tells the full story.

DAY 77

The 11 Laws of Hardwiring New Leadership Habits: Law #9

Hardwiring is reinforced when the Nine Box Grid is used to reward those in the upper right while deciding whether to retrain, reassign, or release and replace those consistently in the lower left.

The 11 Laws of Hardwiring New Leadership Habits: Law #10

Professional development is more about progress and less about perfection.

The 11 Laws of Hardwiring New Leadership Habits: Law #11

Hardwiring is enhanced when the developing leader takes time for additional stakeholder feedback and ongoing personal reflection to assess progress and to identify changes needed in the next iteration of learning and application.

Leader-Ship

Leader — Casts vision, models values, inspires, aligns, coaches, delegates, and holds team members accountable.

Ship — The relation-ship with each follower on your team with the goal of building trust and respect essential in any healthy and high performing team that fulfills the organizational strategy.

Leader-Ship leverages positive interpersonal skills to accomplish the daily mission on the way to achieving the ultimate vision.

DAY 81

The Public Domain of Your Non-Verbals

Body language speaks more loudly than your spoken words, telling others what you actually mean.

DAY 82

Leaders Are on a Developmental Journey

Who you **were** doesn't have to be who you **are**, and …

Who you **are** doesn't have to be who you can **become**.

MARCH

Getting the Work Done

Leaders used to do the work. Now they see to it that the work gets done … by others.

MARCH

DAY 84

Expectation Exceeders, Meeters, and Missers

If you are a leader who is generally the **Expectation Exceeder** in surpassing the assignments from your boss, then you might have a tendency to communicate to the **Expectation Meeters** on your team that they are always falling short.

It's not fair to impose your perfectionist orientation on those who are doing the job you hired them to do.

The **Expectation Missers**? If you let them persist, then they always lower the productive potential of the entire team.

The Eisenhower Matrix

Avoid the "Urgency" trap.

Prioritize your time on what matters most.

	URGENT	NOT URGENT
IMPORTANT	**Do:** Tasks with deadlines or consequences.	**Schedule:** Tasks with unclear deadlines that contribute to long-term success.
NOT IMPORTANT	**Delegate:** Tasks that must get done but don't require your specific skill set.	**Delete:** Distractions and unnecessary tasks.

DAY 86

Organizational Culture Done Right

A healthy culture is built with others not imposed on others.

Every organizational value is behavioralized.

The behavioral consistency of each value is expected of everyone.

Behavioral miscues, when values are abused, are not tolerated by anyone.

360-degree stakeholder feedback corrects any personal blind spots regarding value consistency.

Onboarding and annual reviews include accountability for the valued behaviors.

DAY 87

The Outline of Leadership

Vision – Where we are headed.

Mission – What we do daily to achieve the ultimate vision.

Values – How we agree to work together in executing the daily mission.

Strategy – The tactical agenda that moves us from mission to vision.

Staffing – Getting people aligned and accountable in doing the right things.

Structure – Leverage staffing models to fulfill the strategy while living out values and executing the mission on the way to achieve the vision.

Systems – Processes used to effectively and efficiently manage organizational resources to achieve strategic objectives.

MARCH

Trickle-Up Leadership

Trickle-up leaders regularly tell each team member how what they do contributes to the vision, mission, values, and strategy of the entire organization.

DAY 89

Parkinson's Law

It is often said that work expands so as to fill the time available for its completion.

... What's your personal application as you consider how your team gets work done?

... What's your "aha" moment in how you get work done?

Action Step: Communicate realistic timelines and follow up with consistent accountability.

MARCH

DAY 90

Leadership Non-Negotiables

To lead others, you must first lead yourself.

To lead yourself, you must first know yourself.

To know yourself:

... What do you value?

... What is your life purpose?

... What are your relational and work strengths?

... What do you want said at the end of your career?

MONTH 04

APRIL

RECALIBRATE YOUR CALLING EVERY DAY

MONTH 04

Translating Vision into Reality

Organizational health is grounded in its culture when the company's values are modeled and practiced consistently. When the value of leadership development addresses both character and competence, it exponentially multiplies the productive potential of every leader, every team, and ultimately the productive potential of the entire organization. That is its capacity.

APRIL

The Culture Cube

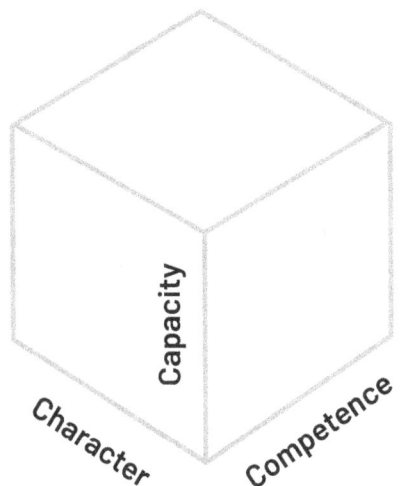

Managing Teams: Step #1

Hire the best you can afford, while paying attention to cultural fit.

Managing Teams: Step #2

Develop each team member in areas needed to achieve their productive potential.

APRIL

Managing Teams: Step #3

Retrain, reassign, or release and replace the continual underperformers.

APRIL

Managing Teams: Step #4

Delegate stretch assignments of the work you should no longer continue to do.

Managing Teams: Step #5

Set team members up for success in delegated assignments for everything they will need.

Managing Teams: Step #6

Never default to past expertise by taking work back from your team in times of stress and pressure.

APRIL

Managing Teams: Step #7

Provide clarity of what success looks like as well as your availability and accessibility.

Managing Teams: Step #8

Establish benchmark check-in points on shared calendars for each delegated assignment.

Managing Teams: Step #9

Let team members fail while you initiate a debrief of learnings for future success.

Managing Teams: Step #10

Celebrate the achievements, reminding each team member how their work contributes to strategic organizational outcomes.

Managing Teams: Step #11

Keep learning how to lead more effectively and efficiently through periodic leadership development coaching informed by feedback from key stakeholders.

Managing Teams: Step #12

Accept these realities:

1. Leadership is a learned competence.

2. Leadership is contextual in agilely adapting to the current needs of the organization.

3. Leadership development is incremental in each iteration of building more effective habits of leading your team.

APRIL

DAY 103

Creating a Culture of "Appreciation"

Gratitude is the power of a thankful leader.

Try saying "Thank you!" more than asking "Will you?"

DAY 104

What to Ask Before You Speak

Should I wait to speak until after I listen to my team?

Will my comment contribute any new information?

What if I delegate this decision to the team member most affected?

Is consensus possible?

How does the risk compare to the potential benefit?

APRIL

DAY 105

Talking the Walk and Walking the Talk

Leadership is not about what you say but what you do once you say it.

Incremental Leadership Development

You can't get better at everything.

You can get better at one thing.

APRIL

DAY 107

Leadership's Great (and Daily) Reveal!

Every day, you start over …

Leading Inside-Out and Outside-In

The **outside** of leadership is what you do.

The **inside** of leadership is who you are.

Collaborative synergy between the inside and the outside is the nonnegotiable for any leader's productive potential.

APRIL

DAY 109

Provocative Leadership Question #1

Are you a step ahead or a step behind your competition? Are you following them, or are they following you? Might you both need to swallow some pride and collaboratively follow each other?

Provocative Leadership Question #2

Do you design your own best practices through an ongoing process of incremental tests of change and iterations of continual improvement? Or do you just accept industry best practices that fit another context but may not be uniquely applicable to your organization?

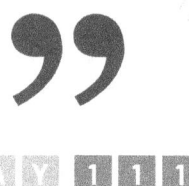

Provocative Leadership Question #3

Do you know the limits of your leadership capacity? Capacity is your ability to lead at higher levels of organizational complexity. Do you know how to manage capacity limits? Are you willing to address competency gaps that have the potential to stall or derail a career?

Provocative Leadership Question #4

Do you know the toxic signs of a team member who has become divisive by undermining your leadership? It's a question of culture loyalty. Watch for these cues: their gossip, rumor, triangulation of other team members against you, becoming more aloof, critical humor, lack of engagement, and the inability to look you in the eye and be vulnerably honest. Too many leaders tolerate toxicity and wait too long to deal directly with the divisive direct report. When you wait to avoid uncomfortable conflict, they win at your expense. The price is team dysfunction and a loss of the organization's productive potential.

APRIL

Provocative Leadership Question #5

Can you say, "I don't know?" Can you say, "I'm sorry?" Can you say, "I was wrong?" Sustainable leaders are willing to take the blame and leverage their mistakes (or the mistakes of others) as teachable moments for the entire team.

Provocative Leadership Question #6

Do you know the cost of justifying your executive rudeness because of your self-perception of importance, busyness, and elite privilege? The "Anybodys" in your organization are "Somebodys." The more you treat them like "Nobodys," the less is their respect, trust, loyalty, engagement, and productivity for you. And, their retention is always in play.

Provocative Leadership Question #7

Do you give credit? How often do you catch someone doing something right and tell them? Do you recognize, reward, and celebrate teams and team members? When is the last time you did it apart from the year-end holiday party? Tell them. Tell others. Don't default to a text or email … ever!

Provocative Leadership Question #8

Are you breaking through organizational silos by aligning teams to shared outcomes with cross-functional strategies through open and transparent communication?

APRIL

Leaders Either *Have* Character or They *Are* Characters

It's impossible to lead effectively for the long haul without the consistency of positive character that all can see. Respect, trust, and loyalty are the return on your investment in character development.

Judging Character

Without the ability to assess the character of others, leaders lack an essential competency needed in every team or organization to determine the correct balance point between over trusting or under trusting the motives of each direct report.

Building Teams

Phase One – Leaders set a direction that clarifies the daily mission leading to the ultimate vision for the organization.

Phase Two – Leaders assemble the best collection of subject matter experts available in light of existing resources.

Phase Three – Leaders develop strategic plans that align and organize the collaboration of individuals for maximum productivity.

APRIL

It's a Matter of Perception

Do you want to change how people perceive you as a leader? Involve them in your own leadership development process by asking for their feedback.

MONTH 05

MAY

MONTH 05

Leading Yourself. Leading Others. Leading the Organization.

LEADERSHIP FOCUS	LEADERSHIP GOAL	LEADERSHIP DEFINITION	LEADERSHIP QUALITY	LEADERSHIP MODEL	LEADERSHIP ACTION
CHARACTER					
Leading yourself	Be authentic	Influence of my positive character	Consistency of my leadership behavior	<u>Being</u> *How* leadership is approached	My leadership presence
COMPETENCE					
Leading others	Be wise	Impact of my effective action	Expertise of my leadership skill	<u>Doing</u> *What* leadership accomplishes	My leadership performance
CAPACITY					
Leading the organization	Be strategic	Boundaries of my leadership ability	Depth of my leadership strength	<u>Knowing</u> *Why* leadership succeeds	My leadership potential

MAY

You cannot lead others if you are unable to lead yourself. You cannot lead the organization if you are unable to lead others. Consider eleven facets in the Leadership Core Matrix describing the simultaneous interplay among these three levels. What may appear to be somewhat linear is actually very dynamic in real time with imperfect people in imperfect organizations.

LEADERSHIP SELF-UNDERSTANDING	LEADERSHIP QUESTION	LEADERSHIP INSIGHTS	LEADERSHIP APPLICATION	LEADERSHIP RESULTS
Who am I?	Do people like me?	Integrity of who I am when everyone is looking and when no one is looking	What behaviors are essential in my leadership practice?	Positive character crosses borders, cultures, genders, and generations.
How good am I?	Do people respect me?	Leadership competence is defined by context, culture, and strategic outcomes.	What competencies are critical in my leadership execution?	Aligning my leadership competency mix to the current or anticipated stage of organizational development
How high can I lead?	Do people trust me?	Capacity in one context does not automatically transfer to a different context	What gaps exist that need to be addressed with a leadership coach to enhance my leadership potential?	Awareness of my season of life & situational factors that may limit my current ability to lead at a higher level of organizational complexity

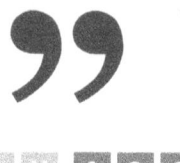

DAY 121

Developmental Cultures

Organizations that value and invest in professional development provide the time, resources, structures, and systems that create a career pathway for every team member.

Getting a Coach

Coaches help team members develop new habits that improve the supervision, management, and leadership of their direct reports.

A Leadership Balancing Act

Leaders are responsible to the organization for outcomes, to the team for alignment and to themselves for work-life balance.

DAY 124

The Publicly Private Practices of Leading

Attitudes Are Perceived.

The core leadership competencies are humility and transparency.

Words Are Interpreted.

The core leadership competencies are clarity and consistency.

Behaviors Are Modeled.

The core leadership competencies are authenticity and approachability.

MAY

DAY 125

Assess Your Bias

| 1 | 2 | 3 | 4 | 5 | 6 | 7 | 8 | 9 | 10 |

TOO CAUTIOUS   TOO RISKY

What is your number? What number would your direct reports give you?

Accomplish the "How To"

Do it …

Delegate it …

Delay it …

Discard it …

MAY

DAY 127

Your Leadership Tells a Story

How you lead tells the story of what you value, of how you see yourself, and of how you see others. Do you like the story you are telling? It's never too late to change the setting, the plot, the characters, the point of view, or the resolution to any conflict.

DAY 128

Memorable Leadership Habits #1: The Visionary Leader

Visionary leaders articulate an inspiring view of what the organization is becoming.

Visionary leaders are committed to the daily mission that one day will lead to vision achievement.

Visionary leaders know that the vision and mission regularly get fuzzy in the minds of team members, and so, revisit the stories that illustrate alignment between the two.

Visionary leaders continually remind each direct report how their work contributes to the mission and ultimately to the vision.

Visionary leaders take time to celebrate each milestone benchmark along the visionary journey.

Visionary leaders are agile and adaptable to adjust their leadership competency priorities as the organization changes.

DAY 129

Memorable Leadership Habits #2: The Communicating Leader

Communicating leaders have the courage to be vulnerable and transparent in their communication.

Communicating leaders tell the same message to every team member with clarity, consistency, and brevity.

Communicating leaders understand how they communicate is more powerful than what they say.

Communicating leaders use stories to communicate complex ideas in understandable terms.

Communicating leaders realize the need to communicate key ideas seven times in seven different ways.

Communicating leaders ask more than they tell in order to listen to honest feedback at all levels.

Communicating leaders believe that there are no dumb questions, so they are timely and responsive to whatever is asked by anyone.

DAY 130

Memorable Leadership Habits #3: The Values-Driven Leader

Values-Driven leaders identify the guardrails that shape organizational culture of how team members ideally work with each other, vendors, customers, investors, and even competitors.

Values-Driven leaders "behavioralize" each value to describe what that ideal looks like in everyday work life.

Values-Driven leaders model the stated ideals in every situation, decision, and interaction as team members rarely go further or faster than their leader.

Values-Driven leaders hire team members who fit the culture reflected in the behaviors represented by each organizational value.

Values-Driven leaders hold team members accountable for the behaviors reflected in the values with immediacy and consistency across the entire team.

Memorable Leadership Habits #4: The Developmental Leader

The Developmental Leader values and invests in the professional development of each direct report.

The Developmental Leader creates pathways for career development to address the what, the why, and the how.

The Developmental Leader conducts "Stay Interviews" with each team member to discuss their career priorities and development pathways.

The Developmental Leader delegates stretch assignments to those ready and equipped to work at higher levels of organizational complexity.

The Developmental Leader is willing to lose team members to new roles in light of their success in building new skills.

Memorable Leadership Habits #5: The Emotionally Smart Leader

The Emotionally Smart leader is learning to be perceptive of all the people and situations that trigger emotional responses.

The Emotionally Smart Leader has learned that awareness of their emotions is only half of the EQ challenge. Managing what one is feeling is the harder of the two steps.

The Emotionally Smart Leader understands that emotional signals go to the feeling side of the brain before going to the thinking side of the brain and have discovered the value of the "pregnant pause" to allow thoughts to catch up to feelings.

The Emotionally Smart Leader owns moments of emotional outburst and clears the air with a genuine and timely apology.

The Emotionally Smart Leader is approachable without expressing "interruption frustration" in all of the body language messages and then commits to attentive listening without interruption.

MAY

The Updated Nine Box Grid

Performance is **past** history.

Potential is a **future** guess.

Personal Drive is a **present** reality.

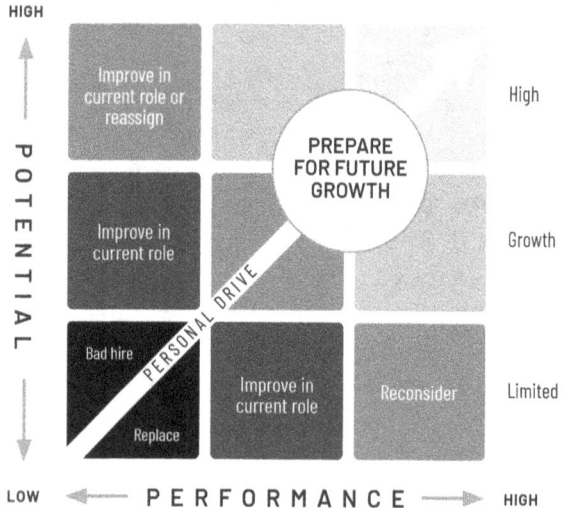

Root Causes of Leadership Dysfunction

Peel away all the self-lies and justification that keep you from the honest reality of what you need to work on next in your professional development journey.

Hiring the Right People for the Right Job

Professional Competence – Do they have the training and experience to do the job effectively and efficiently?

Personal Drive – Do they have the motivation and willingness to do the job well?

Cultural Fit – Will we like them and respect them while they do the job?

Never minimize the significance of their cultural fit!

DAY 136

Leader and/or Friend

There is always a fine line between the **personal** and **professional** in relating to each team member. Be cautious if you consider stepping over that line.

Emotions

Thoughts?

Or Thoughts and Words?

Or Thoughts and Words and Actions?

If you move beyond "thoughts" too quickly, you are more likely to say and do what you will later regret. Wait 24 hours before moving thoughts to words and actions.

Leadership's Strength of Character

Character represents your values in action.

Leadership Give and Take

Gratitude is a leadership investment that we give to others.

Accountability is a leadership withdrawal that we ask from others.

Withdrawals work when investments are made regularly and often.

DAY 140

The Leadership Perception Continuum

| INSECURE | CONFIDENT | ARROGANT |

Leaders are always managing the perceptions of others.

Perceptions are negative at either extreme on the Leadership Presence Continuum.

Accountability Made Easy

Three weekly questions to ask your team:

1. What did you accomplish this week?

2. What challenges interrupted your progress?

3. What are you planning to get done next week?

Defining Progress

The Busyness of Motion

Your continual pace of activity often looks good at first glance. What if busyness isn't accomplishing anything of strategic value?

The Progress of Movement

Your strategic sequence of predetermined activities. What if your movement is efficiently leading toward a strategic outcome?

People work hard to look busy but are they accomplishing anything of value for strategic outcomes? Reward *Movement* and Question *Motion*.

DAY 143

Managing Leadership Time

Only Handle It Once

Process Improvement finds ways to do workflows faster and better. The more times you touch the same email or text, the more time you lose in maximizing your limited work hours.

Procrastination minimizes productivity!

Busy? Try categorizing messages. Drag and drop them into priority-marked folders.

Day 144

Leadership Fears

Do you fear failure?

Why? Will you do it again?

Do you fear success?

Why? Can you do it again?

DAY 145

Strategic Leadership: Critical Thinking

Analyze

Synthesize

Test

Observe

Evaluate

Which step(s) of the critical thinking process should you get better at?

What will you do to get better at it?

When It's Time for Another Meeting

Three Roles That Improve Meeting Outcomes

#1. Who is your Meeting Leader?

They facilitate discussion with attention to group dynamics.

#2. Who is your Meeting Facilitator?

They manage the agenda and the clock.

#3. Who is your Meeting Scribe?

They capture the meeting action items including: What, Who, When.

DAY 147

Listening Is the Other Half of Communication

Intentional listening is the commitment to understand without interruption or judgment.

DAY 148

Two Questions for Your Direct Reports

#1. What do I need to know from you today?

#2. If you could change anything, what would you change?

DAY 149

There Is No Strategic Leadership Without Thinking Time

Great leaders schedule it and block their calendar, without exception.

What would happen if you scheduled Thinking Time every other Friday morning?

How Do You Feel?

The leader who has empathy has connection and influence.

Organizational Politics

Once teams admit they lack adequate resources to be effective and efficient, then the internal competition for a larger share of the operational budget begins. That's politics!

MONTH 06

JUNE

RECALIBRATE YOUR CALLING EVERY DAY

MONTH 06

Leading in Ethical Dilemmas

Behavior is ten times more important in demonstrating leadership character than mere words when leaders are in the intersection of ethical crossroads. Four styles of leadership are pictured in the Ethical Leader Matrix. A code of ethics is foundational to demonstrating one aspect of leadership character. A code establishes behavioral expectations for the leader as well as the team. That code offers the power of advanced decision-making before you find yourself in any ethical dilemma.

JUNE

Ethical Leader Matrix

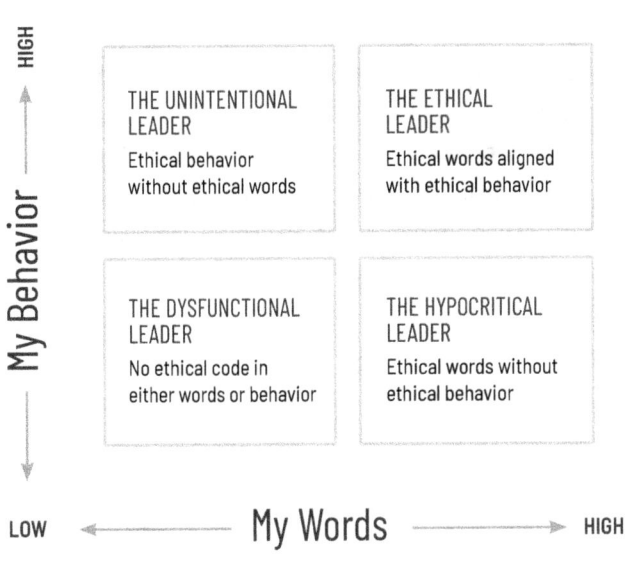

Mid-Level Leaders

Leaders who blame "management" in order to avoid looking like the bad leader lose respect from their team and from "management." Own your role in honestly communicating the what, the how, and the why that may have been decided by others.

Four Ways to Decide

1. The leader listens to the discussion and makes the decision.

2. The leader facilitates discussion with the goal of consensus.

3. The leader facilitates discussion and the majority rules.

4. The leader facilitates discussion and delegates the final decision to the team member who owns the outcome.

Leaders tell the team how the decision will be made before the meeting begins.

The "First Step" Rule of Procrastination

Immediately complete the first step in any new assignment.

... Create the timeline.

... Identify the steps to completion.

... Schedule each step.

... Do step #1.

DAY 155

Creating a Civil Workplace

It's at the heart of organizational culture.

It's stated in company values.

It's modeled from the top down.

It's expected from the bottom up.

It's addressed in immediate feedback when it's missing.

It's recognized and celebrated whenever it's demonstrated.

The Rhythm of Every Meeting

What is the agenda?

Why is it important to meet?

Who needs to attend?

When is it scheduled?

Where are we meeting?

How long do we need to meet?

Do I need to attend, or can someone represent me?

When Strategic and Tactical Clash

Sometimes the square peg doesn't fit the round hole.

Leadership wisdom is having the discernment and discretion to admit it's time to go back to the drawing board with input from every key stakeholder. The "Iceberg of Ignorance" suggests that many executive leaders actually know little of what is below the waterline of the iceberg because they don't ask or listen to all levels of employment.

Start asking. Start listening. Start valuing feedback.

Understanding the Context of Strategy

The SWOT Analysis – The factors that define your marketplace position.

Strengths, Weaknesses, Opportunities, Threats

The QUEST Analysis – The trends and market conditions affecting your options.

Quick, Environmental, Scanning, Technique

The PEST Analysis – The big picture of your context.

Political, Economic, Social, Technological

The best leaders understand the context in which their company operates.

Brainstorming Tools for Your Team

Think out of the box. No bad ideas. No judgement. Build on other's ideas.

Space: Go to an unlikely and uninterrupted place to focus and think freely.

Questions: Why not? What if? Risk/Benefit? Worse-case scenario?

Workflow: What's the logical sequence of steps from here to there?

Pictures: How is our question/dilemma similar to what you see in this picture?

Story: Start a story that is added to by each participant and describes the ideal outcome: "I see the day when we..."

JUNE

When Plan "A" Doesn't Work

Leadership is about your readiness, willingness, and adaptability to execute "Plan B"

I'm Leading. What could go wrong?

YOU ...

... At your most vulnerable moment.

... In your weakest area of leadership competency.

Let's be honest. Maybe it's time for you to face the leadership music and change the key you keep playing in. Do yourself and your team and your organization a favor – get a leadership coach and rewrite your leadership opus.

JUNE

Is Leadership a Laughing Matter?

| 1 | 2 | 3 | 4 | 5 | 6 | 7 | 8 | 9 | 10 |

DOESN'T DARE 　　　　　　　　　　 CANNOT WAIT

The Leadership-Laughter Continuum

#1. Your team doesn't dare laugh at you............
#10. Your team cannot wait to laugh at you.

Laughter is essential to healthy organizational culture. Leaders are the key to a culture of humor. Model it. Offer it. Take it.

DAY 163

The Making of a Leader

The Mind of a Leader – The ability to approach every person and every situation with discernment, discretion, judgement, and strategy.

The Heart of a Leader – The attitude of humility in modeling the values that define the culture of an organization in every word and action.

The Hands of a Leader – A choice to collaborate with others at any level of the organization and align all resources toward shared outcomes.

The Feet of a Leader – The willingness to lead while always walking in the shoes of those who follow.

Leadership Mistakes and Success

Leaders own their mistakes.

Respected and trusted leaders accept the consequences of their mistakes, make things right, and then choose to never lead in that way again.

Leaders share their success.

Respected and trusted leaders disperse the credit, collaboratively analyze the process, and then leverage the insights for future leadership best practice.

Directional Clarity

The leader's ability to cast vision regarding the right outcomes, at the right time, in the right way, for the right reasons, and to the right audience.

JUNE

The First Commitment of Any Leader

To consistently model the behavioral implications of all organizational values in every attitude, word, and action.

Strategy Defined

The skill to think in reverse from potential deliverable outcomes to present realities and devise a sequential plan to move from today to a new tomorrow.

DAY 168

Team Building Simplified

When leaders are willing to recruit, equip, engage, and delegate to team members whose strengths compensate for and complement their own non-strength areas.

Leadership Intelligence

The anticipation of expected issues inherent in each stage of the organizational development lifecycle. The ability to predict and explain each challenge and the willingness to let any employee be part of the solution.

When You Blow It, Let Mistakes Be the Shortest Route to Success

Welcome mistakes as part of your leadership development journey.

Admit mistakes to build transparency, integrity, credibility, and trust.

Identify the "mistake lessons" to determine how not to make the same mistake again.

Pay it forward by sharing your imperfect journey with other emerging leaders in order to shorten their learning curve.

Organizational Culture

Leaders intentionally create interpersonally healthy places to work for every team member, not just for themselves.

JUNE

Leadership Formation

Building leaders incrementally from the outside in and from the inside out.

JUNE

DAY 173

The Pace of the Leader

Team members will rarely go further or faster than their leader.

A Strategic Mindset

The intuition of leadership judgement must be inherently strategic in achieving stated outcomes.

The Daily Agenda of Leading

The ability, clarity, and creativity of casting vision of a better tomorrow by honestly addressing the realities of today and the gap that exists in between.

DAY 176

When Is a Team a Healthy Team?

When collaborative and cross-functional alignment is possible, a healthy team can become a high performing team.

Followership

Those who have absolute clarity on their role and assignment and commit daily to engagement, satisfaction, and loyalty in spite of imperfect leaders, team members, and organizational culture.

Communication

Messaging is effective when everyone knows everything they need to know in a consistent and timely way.

Questions to Ask on Your Career Path

The Attraction Question
Do I want to work for this organization?

The Culture Question
Is this company intentionally accelerating leadership development?

The Assessment Question
Do I have the capacity to lead at higher levels of organizational complexity?

The Retention Question
Am I growing in the areas of leadership competency needed in this company?

The Succession Question
Is there an opportunity for my career advancement in the leadership succession plan?

JUNE

Organizational Culture and Climate

Leaders Drive Culture — The values-driven ideal of how team members are expected to work together to achieve strategic goals.

Followers Shape Climate — Determined by the consistency of values lived out in attitudes, words, and behaviors by every team member every day.

Effective Leadership – Closing the gap between culture and climate.

The Trust Formula

Integrity + Respect + Consistency

Integrity – The perception others have of you.

Respect – The perception you have of others.

Consistency – The perception by team members that your public self matches your private self, and your perception that their public self matches their private self.

MONTH 07

JULY

MONTH 07

Leading Each Direct Report Differently

There is a difference between building a team and building up a team. Leading is the responsibility of meeting each direct report at their point of greatest need whether it is the need for more encouragement and recognition or the need for a greater degree of challenge and accountability. The goal of either is to motivate the team member towards their full potential. Getting the task done while supporting the team member is that delicate balance that can change daily and even moment by moment.

JULY

It's a Balancing Act

 TASK

Who Trusts Whom?

Trust is the foundation of effective leadership.

Trust is the non-negotiable of high-performing teams.

... It's the trust of the team by the leader.

... It's the trust of the leader by the team.

Building Blocks

Vision – The driving statement of what the company is becoming.

Leaders cast vision in compelling ways.

Mission – The daily work that leads to achieving the vision.

Leaders share stories to illustrate how the mission is being lived out.

Values – The beliefs that guide and shape every attitude, word, and behavior.

Leaders model the behaviors reflecting the values that define culture.

When Leaders Live Values

Leaders define values.

Leaders tie values to strategic outcomes

Leaders model values in attitudes, words, and behaviors.

Leaders notice and encourage values in action.

Leaders hold every team member accountable to shared values.

Leaders give immediate and consistent feedback when values are missed.

Organizational Framework

Strategy – Best practice approach to move from current state to the desired future state.

Structure – The most effective and efficient way to organize and maximize organizational resources.

Staffing – Adapting to changes needed for the structure to be successful by retraining, reassigning, or releasing and replacing.

Systems – Processes that streamline the strategic approach to optimize performance throughout the company.

How Leaders Shape Culture

Declare it!

Define it!

Model it!

Defend it!

Expect it!

Measure it!

Reward it!

DAY 187

Levels of Leadership

The emerging leader — manages a team.

The mid-level leader — leads managers.

The senior leader — leads leaders.

The strategic leader — leads the enterprise.

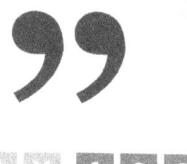

Assessing Direct Reports

Performance – Objectively measured by missing, meeting, or exceeding goals.

Potential – Perceived ability to handle increasing organizational complexities.

Personal Drive – Ability and willingness to develop personal competency gaps while taking on stretch assignments with escalated responsibility.

DAY 189

A Leader's Capacity

The ability and readiness to lead at higher levels of organizational complexity determined by:

Unique Wiring – A leader's strengths and competency profile.

Season of Life – Personal realities that define one's work-life balance.

Personal Drive – Having a career plan with professional aspirations.

Professional Opportunity – Delegated stretch assignments.

Intentional Learning – Application of new insights as a lifelong learner.

Accountable Coaching – A skilled leadership coach monitors, measures, and manages a professional development growth plan.

Defining Terms

Capacity – The ability to lead at a specific level of organizational responsibility.

Development – The life-long commitment of learning to lead more effectively and efficiently.

Leadership – The combination of positive influence ("I like you") and effective action ("I respect you").

DAY 191

Setting the Stage for Delegation

The Delegation Challenge. Leaders can't take on a more strategic role until offloading some of what they keep doing operationally that someone else could and should be doing.

The Delegation Question. What can I delegate? When, how, and to whom?

The Delegation Process.

Step #1 – Watch me, and then let's discuss what you observed.

Step #2 – Let's do it together, and then let's discuss what you experienced.

Step #3 – Let me watch you do it, and then let's discuss what I observed.

Step #4 – Now you do it on your own, and then let's discuss how it's going.

JULY

DAY 192

Organizational Core Competencies

Have you identified four to six core leadership competencies, skills, or behaviors that uniquely define your company's "Leadership Competency Profile?"

This profile represents the leadership skills needed to achieve the productive potential of every team member, leading to the fulfillment of strategic outcomes while sustaining corporate values.

JULY

DAY 193

How Can I Develop Further?

Once you have identified a few focus areas for your professional development through research-based assessments and feedback from key stakeholders ...

Think – What do you need to learn about each focus area?

Talk – Discuss how your learning applies with a coach or colleague.

Act – Apply two or three incremental action steps from your conversation.

Reflect – Get feedback from your team about your progress.

DAY 194

Accelerate Leadership Development

1. What core competencies are needed by every leader?
2. Are you building an internal talent pool to fill open roles?
3. Is there a strategy to attract and retain leadership talent?
4. Are you satisfied with the outcomes of your current system?
5. Is leadership development aligned to outcomes and values?
6. What risk do you face if a key leader leaves or retires?
7. Have you considered the time and cost to onboard a new leader?
8. Do you have a succession model and plan for all levels of key leaders?

JULY

The Always-Never Questions

Values are behaviors to live, not just ideas to believe.

Example: We value the respect of every individual.

Question #1: If we want to have a culture of respect, what should we always do?

Question #2: If we want to have a culture of respect, what should we never do?

Five Trust Multipliers

It takes time to build trust through the routine ways of responding to the opportunities and obstacles of each day.

Honesty – The opposite of lies, exaggeration, partial truth, deception, and cover up.

Commitments – Never promise unless you intend to follow through.

Transparency – No hidden agendas or deals under the table.

Clarity – Avoid spin, confusing answers, and long explanations.

Consistency – When every team and every team member hears the same message.

DAY 197

The Emotional Sequence

Trigger – Life experiences initiate positive and negative emotions.

Reaction – We respond out of our emotional repertoire.

Consequence – How we choose to react emotionally in these moments impacts everyone around us positively or negatively.

Emotional Intelligence (EQ) - The awareness and management of our emotions. Letting the thinking side of the brain catch up to the feeling side of the brain protects leaders from negative consequences.

The Emotional Matrix

DAY 199

The Emotional Question

Is this the best time, place, person, and level of intensity to express what I am feeling in this moment?

DAY 200

The Danger of the 15%

Some leaders are often right. It's a powerful gift to be a subject matter expert and be right even 85% of the time. The danger is when a leader assumes they are right 100% of the time. It becomes an interpersonal blind spot 15% of the time when they are wrong but think they are right.

Predicting Change

Leaders bring clarity by predicting what change is coming, and they explain reasons behind the needed change.

What needs to be communicated regarding why the change is critical?

When is the best time to communicate for optimum understanding?

Where should it be delivered so everyone hears the same message?

How is the message crafted so key questions are answered?

Why is this change important now?

The "How to" of Leading Change

Three Leadership Movements

1. Preparation – Continuous change necessitates a communication plan and the identification of resources needed.

2. Implementation – The moment of change rarely occurs without complications. That's when all the critics come out of the woodwork!

3. Transition – The change event is never as disruptive as the transition that follows. Leaders assist each wave of adopting to the new change.

DAY 203

Strategic Leadership: Make an Appraisal of Where the Organization is Today

Collect – What should you keep, stop, start or change doing?

Organize – Identify the categories of feedback from all levels of employment.

Analyze – Review each category of information to see the story in the data.

Synthesize – Connect the dots of your strengths, weaknesses, and opportunities.

Summarize – The synopsis of where you are and where you need to be.

Current State Future State

Where are you headed?

Picture – Craft an inspiring visual of what the organization will look like when you arrive at your change goal.

Why – What current realities prevent you from settling in and just staying the course?

Assumptions – What guides, informs, supports, and defines the direction you are heading?

DAY 205

Considering Change Options

Articulate the options available and compare each scenario:

Criteria for scenario selection

Effort and Impact of each option

Connection to Stakeholder Groups

Alignment to your Vision, Mission, and Values

Timeline to Reach Your Destination

DAY 206

Looking for the Silver Bullet

Leaders would love a guaranteed quick solution for difficult problems.

There are no quick fixes for complex issues.

Start by looking for the root cause. That just might be the silver bullet.

Three Kinds of Leaders

Efficient Leaders search for ways to get more done with the same investment of resources.

Expedient Leaders allow the end to justify the means in order to meet deadlines and outcomes.

Effective Leaders never jump to conclusions while crafting a consistent problem-solving approach.

Own Your Leadership Identity

Effective leaders are agilely adaptable in selecting a leadership approach to lead workplace teams toward increased productivity.

Mistake #1: Not knowing your current leadership identity.

Mistake #2: Not understanding what that identity should be in order to meet strategic organizational goals.

Mistake #3: Not willing to pay the price of change.

DAY 209

Leadership Intelligence: Leading the right people to use the right tools, in the right way, at the right time, and for the right results.

Answering the **What** question is foundational to assessing culture.

Answering the **How** question is foundational to thinking strategically.

Answering the **Why** question is foundational to casting the vision.

Hard Skills + Soft Skills

Hard Skills address the bottom line by articulating a clear vision, telling inspiring stories of how of the daily mission leads to that vision, strategizing how to move from today's reality to tomorrow's changes, and aligning all the resources to work collaboratively toward that future goal.

Soft Skills address interpersonal dynamics and the politics of organizational culture by enhancing one's relational savvy, exercising emotional intelligence, connecting diverse networks, operating with openness and transparency, and demonstrating and supporting a healthy work-life balance.

A Leader's Most Valuable Asset

Your most precious resource is not what you know or what you can do, but how you use your time.

The two leadership time challenges:

Leadership Challenge #1: Protecting your time to do the most important assignments rather than the urgent interruptions.

Leadership Challenge #2: Managing the time you protect to identify efficiencies through process improvement initiatives.

JULY

The Pareto Principle on Priorities

Otherwise known as the 80/20 Rule, 80% of the problems come from 20% of the causes. Address the primary causes in light of the limits of your time to get the greatest impact.

MONTH 08

AUGUST

MONTH

Going Deeper

Sidney Yoshida studied the leadership habits of Japanese car manufacturer, Calsonic in 1989. He coined the phrase "Iceberg of Ignorance" as a reminder that the higher up you are in leadership the less you really know about what is happening below the surface. Exemplary leaders find ways to listen to team members at all levels of employment.

AUGUST

The Iceberg of Ignorance

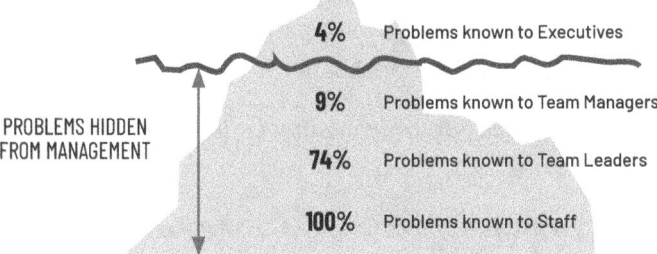

What Are Your Top Priorities?

The Four-Category Solution

A Priorities – Things you must get done today during your best work hours.

B Priorities – Things you will get to by the end of the week.

C Priorities – Things you need to delegate to a team member who has the readiness, skills, and resources to take that assignment off your hands.

D Priorities – Things you discard that don't need to be touched again.

AUGUST

Executives Execute

Any gap between strategy and outcomes is at the point of implementation. The execution gap always inhibits goal achievement and organizational performance.

Strategy + Execution = Outcomes

AUGUST

DAY 215

When Do You Stop Leading?

You stop leading when you stop learning, growing, changing, listening, encouraging, confronting, celebrating, delegating, studying the competition, remembering the customer, dreaming, and taking on the next challenge.

New Hires

The hiring process suggests six selection criteria: Competency, Compatibility, Chemistry, Character, Compensation, and Call. Weight each one in selecting your best candidate.

Dysfunctional Team Member?

Assess the reasons for being out of step with the values.

Find out if they are aware of their value gap.

Ask if they understand the significance of the disparity.

Discuss their willingness to engage with the value expectations.

Weigh their answer and its impact on the team.

Determine the appropriate response, and do not delay taking action.

DAY 218

Why Not Collaborate?

Our differences often begin with a win-lose approach that dictates competition rather than collaboration. It's a short-sighted approach with an arrogant goal of going faster and further than the other person. The long-term view of collaboration understands that we accomplish more together than we ever will working apart.

That's when we bring two ideas, two perspectives, two approaches, two processes, two outcomes and an exponential number of new ideas in our best brainstorming discussions. Embracing differentness enhances the chance of getting to a win-win approach.

Counterintuitive Conflict

Counterintuitive suggests that an idea appears to be the opposite of what one would expect. Leaders often back away from the tensions created by conflict with a team member or conflict between team members. How about modeling a culture that values conflict but limits it to ideas rather than conflict between individuals? That's counterintuitive!

Identify common ground.

Build on the positive.

Gain consensus on ground rules.

Negotiate the conversation.

Agree to disagree when necessary.

Give and take does not imply a winner and a loser.

Celebrate a shared win.

Cooperation or Collaboration

Co-lab-o-ra-tion literally means to co-labor or to labor together with other team members.

... Cooperation is working **with** others to enable them to complete an activity or assignment.

... Collaboration is working **alongside** other team members to accomplish something together that would not otherwise have happened.

It takes time.

It's messy.

It necessitates a skilled facilitator.

It begs for clarity.

It's worth it.

Leadership and Followership

Leaders do not exist without followers, and followers necessitate leadership. When leaders and followers work in harmony, the rhythm fosters growth and greater productivity not otherwise attainable.

DAY 222

Intertwining of Personal and Professional

Leaders tend not to be "Happy Hour" friends with team members, but there are moments when the leader has the opportunity to stand with a team member whose world is overcome by life's messiness. It is the choice to step from the professional into the personal. In this human side of leadership, the risks are immense, but the rewards are immeasurable.

AUGUST

DAY 223

When You Meet with Your Team

Ignoring the group dynamics when your team meets is a leadership oversight. Facilitation of any meeting is a learned skill. Most don't take time to learn and, as a result, don't do it well. Meetings are the most dreaded part of anyone's workday. Learn to have great meetings and you leverage the power of Aristotle's statement that the whole is greater than the sum of its parts.

When Meetings Lack Purpose

Is your next meeting for the purpose of informing or deciding?

... Clearly identify the deliverable that will result from each meeting.

... When your agenda announces the question ahead of time, then team members can come with advanced consideration and preparation for the time they are investing in each meeting.

... Defer any ideas outside your purpose or outcome to a "Parking Lot" list for future review and prioritization.

AUGUST

DAY 225

Leaders Assess Readiness

Leaders communicate different messages to different team members who are at different points of readiness for stretch assignments.

Invest in Leadership Development

Consider the Return on Investment (ROI) from an accelerated leadership development program. The organizational impact includes talent attraction, employee engagement, employee satisfaction, increased productivity, healthy organizational culture, and the retention of your high-potential employees.

AUGUST

The Sequence of Change

Change the individual and you change the organization. Change the organization and you create organizational resilience that serves your employees, customers, vendors, and your investors for the next chapter in the organizational lifecycle.

Strategy or Strategic

Strategy is a noun.

Strategic is an adjective.

Having a strategy and leading strategically are not the same.

DAY 229

The Leadership Toolbox

Is your toolbox expanding to include a medley of approaches that allow you to agilely adjust your leadership style to meet the current needs of a changing organization?

DAY 230

Are You Improving Your Leadership?

What is the most important skill, competency, or leadership behavior that needs further development?

... Start understanding it, valuing it more, and applying it consistently.

... Ask for feedback from those closest to you at work. Are they seeing any change?

DAY 231

Expectations and Accountability

Accountability for those who follow is essential for leaders and team members. It does not suggest micromanagement. It is the means to ensure a common understanding of the status of any project. Clarity of expectations includes:

Outcome

Timeline

Benchmarks

Check-in Points

Day 232

Underperformers

They can be ignored, tolerated, developed, reassigned, or released and replaced. Leaders know who they are, what to do, and when to do it. If you ignore or tolerate them, they will never raise the bar. They only undermine the productive potential of every other team member. If you wait for the problem to go away, it never does. The longer you wait, the greater the cost to the bottom line, to engagement, and to retention of other valuable employees.

Two Reasons for Disengagement

Personal Baggage

Life offers its toughest challenges at the most inopportune times of one's career development. The baggage created by difficult seasons often interferes with an employee's full engagement at work.

Organizational Dysfunction

Companies are flawed as imperfect people lead and follow in the competition for limited resources. As a result, an employee's engagement moves from confusion to frustration to criticism to cynicism to total disengagement.

Seven Times Seven Ways: How Leaders Master Communication

Repeat! Repeat! Repeat!

Sequence Your Communication Flow.

Simplicity Keeps it Simple.

Clear and Concise.

What's the Sale You Are Making?

Consistency Counts.

Don't Cry Wolf.

DAY 235

Redundancy

Leaders communicate clearly, concisely, and redundantly. Their most influential tool is the choice to put critical ideas into words time and time again. Even more important than words are word pictures.

Tell a story.

Let a team member tell their story.

Start a story and let the room add to it or analyze it.

Use an analogy or metaphor.

Do You Have a Question?

Compelling communication has two facets, and one is more important than the other. Both require continued practice, new learning, and more practice.

Profound communicators invest more effort in learning to ask powerful questions than in giving the right answer.

The leadership rule: Ask 51% of the time and Tell 49% of the time.

The Leader as Career Coach

The Society for Human Resource Management's idea of the "Stay Interview" suggests that each supervisor, manager, or leader initiate conversations with every direct report regarding their career plan and career pathway.

It's a focused one-on-one.

Ask questions to explore their career planning.

Provide thoughtful and intentional support and advocacy for each team member.

Allow work time for professional development.

Four Declarations of Every Leader

The world of Hospice care reminds us to not wait too long to say four statements in our relationships. It applies at work too:

Thank You
A culture of gratitude.

I'm sorry
A culture of humility.

I love (appreciate) you
A culture of esteem.

Good Bye
A culture of transitions.

AUGUST

DAY 239

Succeeding at Succession Planning

Initiate an intentional and ongoing process to identify future leadership additions and potential transitions.

Use leadership development initiatives that move team members from a larger talent pool into a leadership pipeline for readiness of new opportunities.

DAY 240

Recognize - Reward - Celebrate

The Law of Recognition – Someone is noticing, remembering, and recognizing.

The ROI for recognition is productivity and job satisfaction.

The Law of Reward – Given privately to those who exceed expectations.

The ROI for Rewards is productivity and engagement.

The Law of Celebration – For teams who have successfully achieved or surpassed goals.

The ROI for Celebration is productivity and retention.

The Test of Leadership

A test of leadership capacity is one's ability to emotionally withstand the subtle and sometimes overt hostility to your leadership.

Criticism – The disapproving attitude from team members who assume they know more and are better than you.

Challenge – The defiant attitude of a team member who wants your position and will disagree with most of what you do and how you do it.

Gossip – The somewhat truthful ideas about you that are inappropriately shared publicly and privately.

Rumor – The false information someone has conjured up to imply that you are over your head and may not know what you are doing.

DAY 242

Values Culture Climate Leadership

Values define how the team members work together.

Culture defines the behaviors behind the values.

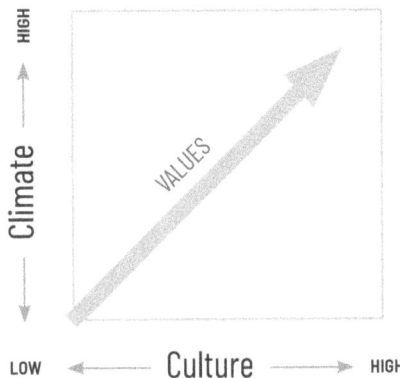

Climate defines how well the behaviors are lived out.

Leadership closes the gap between culture and climate.

DAY 243

The Company and the Leader

The Company's Story

Organizations are always developing.

The Leader's Story

Individuals are always developing.

MONTH 09

SEPTEMBER

MONTH

Personal Reflection and Accountability

Reviewing what you are learning about your own development leads to intentionality in application. This is when you own the responsibility for your personal career planning and professional development. No one will do it for you. Assessing yourself on the ten categories of the Hardwiring Calculation tool will help you objectively review your progress to date. Remember you are focused on progress not perfection. That implies that professional growth is manageable given the need for work-life balance. Each iteration of hardwiring new leadership habits leads to another round of learning and application. The compounding effect for lifelong learners takes the long term view not giving into the quick fix of short term thinking.

SEPTEMBER

A Hardwiring Calculation:

How Sustainable Are Your New Leadership Habits?

① ② ③ ④ ⑤ ⑥ ⑦ ⑧ ⑨ ⑩

Only external learning opportunities	— or —	Numerous internal learning opportunities
I learn just to know more	— or —	I incrementally apply what I learn
What is a career plan?	— or —	I have a career plan
Mission/Vision are management's idea	— or —	What I do contributes to the mission and vision
My values don't match the org's values	— or —	I'm committed to our org's values
I am in the lower left of Nine Box Grid	— or —	I am in the upper right of the Nine Box Grid
I don't fit in with the culture here	— or —	The culture fits my values, motives, & preferences
No development conversations	— or —	Regular proactive development conversations
I never like getting feedback	— or —	I have a few colleagues whom I ask and listen to
The list to work on is too long	— or —	I focus on a few things for incremental development

Blind Spots on the Johari Window

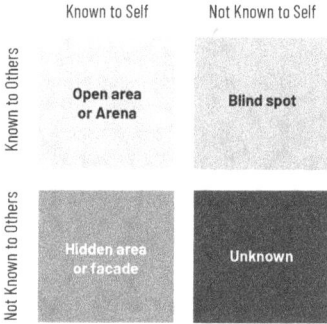

The Johari Window Model

Blind spots get in the way of your leadership until you have the courage to be vulnerable in asking others for honest feedback. When you ask then listen and respond to them. Team members are investing in the next iteration of your professional development whenever you ask for their feedback or feedforward.

Leaders Have Emotions

Emotionally smart leaders will generally outplay their IQ in much of life. Managing emotions is the EQ challenge in the chaos of organizational life.

Emotions. Own them. Accept them as normal. Recognize what triggers them. Identify the intensity of what you're feeling. Consider how rationally you will be perceived if you express that intensity. Determine if this is the time to express them if at all. Reflect how well you are managing them at the end of each day.

The Humility Audit – Part A

Q #1 – Are you a lifelong learner or do you know everything you need to know?

Q #2 - Are you secure enough to consistently model humility?

Q #3 – If you often have strong feelings about work issues, are you aware that you might be wrong? Is it more important that you are perceived as being right?

Q #4 – Do you say "I" more than "We?"

Q #5 – Do you tell more or ask more?

The Humility Audit – Part B

Q #6 – Do you trust your team enough to delegate things they could/should do, knowing that they might do it differently or even better?

Q #7 – Do you tend to give the credit? Do you also take the blame?

Q #8 – When people disagree with you, is your first instinct to listen for understanding, considering that you might have something to learn from them?

Q #9 – Are you an inclusive leader who embraces a diversity of thinking with varying points of view?

Q #10 – Do you realize that your confidence may be perceived as arrogance?

Forging Character Through Failure

Failure may seem like the end of your leadership. It may lead to some endings, but that doesn't prevent a new beginning. A "do over" always starts with reflection:

1. What was I thinking?

2. Own the what and the why.

3. Accept the consequences.

4. Redefine yourself.

5. Recycle the pain to the benefit of your team.

DAY 249

Failure's Four Lessons

1. Create a team culture where failure is expected and allowed as part of the journey to success.

2. Provide a pathway for failure recovery.

3. Discuss the failure with the team member. Ask the first "why" of what is behind the failure. Then ask "why" again and again and again in order to fully explore the cause-and-effect relationships that underlie what happened.

4. Identify insights that will help you build on the failure as a step toward success that avoids repeating the same mistake another time.

When Did You Last Fail?

What was the biggest failure that led you to a new beginning?

Owning and learning from your failure builds integrity and respect in how you see yourself and how others see you.

Identity – Perception – Reputation

Identity – Who you think you are.

Perception – Who others think you are.

Reputation – The interpretation others make from their perception of you.

... Liking you is all about interpersonal chemistry and common ground.

... Respecting you is the recognition of your competence at work.

Reputation is strengthened when liking you and respecting you are aligned.

SEPTEMBER

DAY 252

Who Are Your Peers?

Are your peers competitors or collaborators?

Do you network internally to get to know your peers?

What percentage of time do you initiate collaboration?

DAY 253

C-Suite Team Group Thinking

How do you keep your ear to the ground to listen to every level of employment?

DAY 254

Misalignment?

What happens when you are out of alignment with the organization?

… How long can you stay?

… When will the company see the misalignment?

… Do you have enough influence to attempt culture change?

… When should you leave?

DAY 255

Empathy or Sympathy?

Leading with one's **heart**: Empathy—Feeling what someone else feels from their perspective.

Leading with one's **head**: Sympathy—Understanding what someone else feels from your perspective.

When you choose, mostly choose empathy.

SEPTEMBER

DAY 256

Employee Engagement and Employee Satisfaction

Are you engaged but not satisfied?

Are you satisfied but not engaged?

Are you neither engaged or satisfied?

What happens when you are both?

The Last Laugh

Resilience is the ability to rise above the scorn of others in a moment of personal or professional failure. When you do, you may get the last laugh.

What Is Your Ethical Code?

A code of ethics is foundational to a leader's integrity. It's all about character.

A personal ethics code defines acceptable behavior.

A personal ethics code is a reference point for self-assessment.

A personal ethics code provides a framework for thinking through biases.

A personal ethics code sets a standard for leadership integrity.

A personal ethics code protects your character.

A personal ethics code gives the power in ethical crossroads by advance decision making.

Nuances of Ethical Leadership

What is your combination between ethical words and ethical behaviors?

The Dysfunctional Leader – No ethical code in word or behavior.

The Unintentional Leader – Ethical behavior without ethical words.

The Hypocritical Leader – Ethical words without ethical behavior.

The Ethical Leader – Ethical words aligned with ethical behavior.

Values and ethical choices are the calling card of integrity for leaders of positive character.

Need a Do-Over?

If you could rewind the calendar and rework an ethical dilemma, what would you do differently? How would it have changed the final decision and outcome? How can you be more informed next time in order to avoid wanting a do-over?

Meet Your Critic

Leadership is never about a legacy of popularity. Critics come in all sizes and shapes with different agendas. It's not a matter of "if" you will have leadership critics but "when."

Be confident in your calling.

Take the initiative to meet the opponent.

Listen with an open mind.

Lead boldly with humility.

Focus more on being respected than being liked.

If you try to keep everyone happy, you never will, and you won't be either.

SEPTEMBER

DAY 262

A Civil Workplace

… Leaders shape organizational culture which is defined by shared values. This is your ideal scenario.

…. Team members determine the organizational climate. This is the daily reality of the workplace experience for every employee.

… The gap between the ideal and the real is the result of toxic personalities, poor leadership, stressful timelines, lack of adequate resources, personal baggage, and an absence of connecting the work of each employee to the mission and vision of the company.

… The leadership challenge is to define how wide the gap is and how to close the distance between the ideal and the real.

Hierarchical Elitism

Pecking Order is all about dominance among poultry. Some dominate while others just give in because that's the way it is. Pecking order also shows up in the hierarchy of any organization where the higher up you go the more privileges follow your position.

For example: corner offices with windows, working remotely whenever you feel like it, executive dining rooms, assigned and covered parking places, memberships at the club. The benefits abound as you climb the ladder.

Elite leaders can openly talk about travel and expensive toys that those below them may never be able to afford. It contributes to the "have" and "have not" distinctions that corrupt working relationships. In all the informal conversations around work or on virtual calls, the less you need to share may be more than enough.

DAY 264

Thank You

Saying those eight letters contributes to building a culture of gratitude. When leaders are grateful to team members, it drives engagement, loyalty, productivity, retention, and then the attraction of new talent.

What?

Be generous with your gratitude.

How?

Say it in person rather than electronically.

Why?

Saying it out loud demonstrates respect and appreciation for each team member.

Day 265

Clearing the Air

Our attitudes, words, non-verbals, and actions can create relational tensions that become the elephant in the room when not dealt with.

A Leadership Solution

Once a year, schedule an "unfinished business" one-on-one with each of your direct reports to clear the air. It's the opportunity to make things right with those you lead.

Ask and listen. Give them an opportunity to name what has bugged them.

If they misunderstood, their perception is still their reality of who you are.

Admit your mistake(s) and apologize. Start the new year with a clean slate.

If You Have the Gift of Leadership, Then Lead with Diligence

Gift – The role of leadership is a gift given to you by the organization and a gift you give in managing the work of every team member.

Diligence – Your drive to lead more effectively and efficiently is the result of your careful attention and persistence to uniquely lead each of your direct reports.

DAY 267

Nice or Tough

1	4	7
NICE LEADERSHIP		TOUGH LEADERSHIP

Nice or tough? It's not an either/or choice. Both styles are needed on the continuum above at different times for each direct report.

Nice – Reflects your competence in practicing the interpersonal soft skills of leadership.

Tough – Reflects competence in practicing the interpersonal hard skills of leading a team.

DAY 268

Leaders Know ...

They know where they have been.

They know where they are.

They know where they are going.

Do you?

SEPTEMBER

DAY 269

Macro-Managing or Micro-Managing

Every conversation with a direct report is a choice between the two. Both are needed at times, but which one do you do most of the time? Which one would your direct reports say you do most of the time? Is there a difference between your perception and theirs? Err on the side of becoming a Macro-Manager.

SEPTEMBER

DAY 270

Non-Verbal Body Language

What people see is more influential than what they hear.

What you say is not as important as how you say it.

How you say it is not as important as what you do.

DAY 271

The Ultimate Perfectionist

It's never good enough, is it? Imagine how others feel when they never measure up to your expectations? Maybe it's not a fair comparison between your perfectionistic tendencies and their consistent performance in doing exactly what you hired them to do?

The Happy Procrastinator

Why not admit you are a procrastinator?

Why not assess the Return on Investment from procrastinating?

Why not start with a "To Do" list and finish the most important item today?

Strategic Leaders Learn to Look Around the Corner to See What Others Do Not Yet See

To think in reverse from a preferred future state back to current realities requires three calculated maneuvers.

Honest Assessment of Current Realities

Informed Determination of the Preferred or Necessitated Future

Transparent Clarity on the Sequence of Change

MONTH 10

OCTOBER

MONTH 10

The 80-20 Leader

Effective and efficient leaders spend 80% of their time on top 20% of their strategic priorities.

It's the difference between the urgent and the important.

It's the value of delegating everything someone else on your team could and should be doing.

OCTOBER

Prioritizing Work

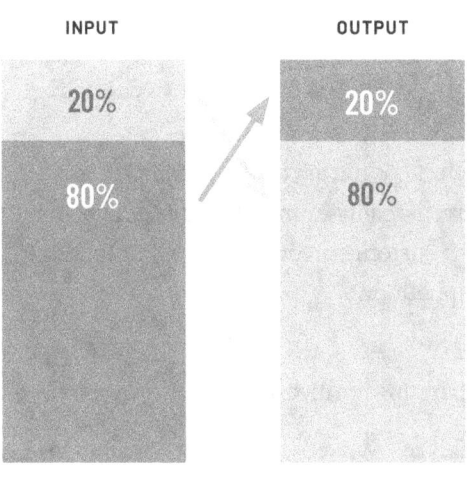

#1 - Create your own master "To Do" list.

#2 - Identify your top three priorities, your bottom three, and then rank the remaining items in middle of your list.

#3 - Your top three represent 20% of work that will get 80% of your time and attention.

#4 - Never hesitate to say "No" If you are asked to take on a project you don't have time for. Ask what you are supposed to let go of to create the margin and time that will be needed.

#5 - Teach your direct reports to prioritize work in the same way you are.

Assessing Organizational Realities

Collect – What are all the versions of your current reality from all levels of employment, your customers, your investors, and your competition?

Organize – Identify the categories of feedback separating positive, negative, and neutral ideas.

Analyze – What themes emerge within the data?

Synthesize – Connect the dots among the themes.

Synopsis – Summarize the story to provide an overview of where you have been, where you are today, and where you need to be in the future.

DAY 275

Unavoidable Realities About Change

1. Change isn't going away.

2. Most don't like it.

3. People adapt on differing timelines.

4. Some resist it as long as possible.

5. The hard work really begins at the moment of change.

6. Those who get on board early are not your best advocates.

7. It's messy and rarely goes as planned.

8. Why is more important than what or how.

DAY 276

Process Improvement

Is every employee part of your process improvement initiative?

How do you collect ideas at all employment levels?

Who leads the review and consideration of ideas suggested?

How do you report on the improvement changes identified?

Do you reward the team or team member who suggested the improvement?

When Culture Is Practiced …

Leaders have three roles in shaping organizational culture.

Identify the values that define the culture.

Model the behaviors implied by the values.

Never tolerate the neglect of those behaviors.

How Agile Are You?

Are you willing to adjust your leadership style to more effectively and efficiently meet the challenges of where the company will be if you achieve the vision?

Communication Subject Matter Expert (SME)

Verbal – Did I do my best to carefully choose my words and how I spoke to them?

Non-Verbal – Did I do my best to ensure that my body language matched my message?

Listening – Did I do my best to genuinely listen for understanding, not agreement?

Written – Did I do my best to craft my ideas in light my audience?

Feedback – Did I do my best to provide positive feedback as well as the negative?

Conflict – Did I do my best to address any tensions with or between team members?

DAY 280

Hiring the Best Patiently

In seasons of talent wars across all industries, hiring the best is hard work. Today's employment opportunities create a challenge in attracting and retaining the best you can afford. Know when you need to wait and keep looking.

Valuing and Investing in Leadership Development

	No Organizational Investment	Organizational Investment
Organizational Value	Inhibits Talent Attraction or Retention	Promotes Leadership Attraction and Retention
No Organizational Value	Leads to Organizational Atrophy	Results in a Trial and Error Approach

DAY 282

The Vulnerability Question for Direct Reports

Am I overmanaging you, or am I undermanaging you?

The Stretch Question for Direct Reports

Are you ready for a new stretch assignment to develop new skills that equip you to lead at higher levels of organizational complexity?

DAY 284

A Menu of Meetings

Moment-in-Time Huddle – A regular catch-up session that is short, sweet, and to the point.

Intentional Benchmark Gathering – The weekly check-in on all action-plan assignments.

Strategic Review and Assessment – Includes monthly updates and plan revisions.

Mission/Vision Appraisal – The annual perspective for strategic plan revisions.

Look-Around-the-Corner Forecast – The three-to-five-year questions of what we need to keep doing, start doing, or stop doing.

DAY 285

Crisis Leadership

Crisis leadership necessitates a prevailing attitude and an innate personal drive to confront the obstacle standing in their way.

Step into the uncertainty and continue leading.

Communicate throughout the crisis.

Empathize authentically.

Clarify what's true.

Be open and accessible.

Phase the way out.

Reflect to capture crisis insights.

OCTOBER

DAY 286

When a New Opportunity is on the Horizon?

Can I?

Do I have the right combination of character and competence required for the new role?

Should I?

Is this the right season in my life to take on a leadership role with greater responsibility?

Must I?

Even if I can, should I pursue or accept a role at a higher level of complexity?

The Perception of Your Executive Presence

Leadership is about influence.

Influence depends on your reputation.

Reputation starts with first impressions.

Executive Presence answers two questions:

1. Do I trust you?

2. Do I respect you?

OCTOBER

DAY 288

How to Ask Questions

Strategic leaders ask the right questions more than having the right answers.

1. *Don't* ask multiple choice questions.

2. *Don't* ask leading questions.

3. *Don't* ask closed questions.

4. *Do* ask your question again in a different way if no answer is immediately given.

5. *Do* repeat the answer you get in your own words to confirm accurate understanding.

6. *Do* follow up with questions that probe deeper.

How Does Your Team See You?

Your work associates quickly decide if they like you and if they respect you. It may not be fair, but how they perceive you impacts how well they follow your lead.

Change their perception and you will change your reputation.

Change your reputation and you will change your influence.

Change your influence and you expand the productive potential of your team.

Do Your Homework

Keep Learning About Yourself

Where are you, where are you going, and what is needed to get there?

Keep Learning About Your Team

What are their interpersonal obstacles that prevent them from high performance?

Keep Learning About Your Organization

Is there alignment among your vision, mission, values, strategy, structure, staffing, and systems?

OCTOBER

DAY 291

Failing Once Again

Own Your Failure

Ask for help if needed. Apologize to everyone touched by your mistake. Make restitutions when it's appropriate. Let it go.

Leverage Your Failure

Design a culture where mistakes and failure are part of the learning process in order to do things differently moving forward.

Avoid Chronic Failure

Repeated failure can be a sign of the wrong person in the wrong position. Is it time for retraining, reassignment, or release and replacement?

Leadership Wandering

When is the last time you scheduled time to walk around your building(s) with the only agenda of noticing, acknowledging, and listening when you ask: "If you could change anything around here, what would you change? Why?"

DAY 293

Strategic Reflection vs. Strategic Planning

1. Schedule a day out of the office.
2. Collect the relevant data before you go.
3. Analyze the data to find the story that emerges.
4. Connect that story to the evaluation of your current reality.
5. Look around the corner to see what others do not yet see about what needs to change.

What do these strategic reflections say about your strategic plan?

Level the Playing Field?

Leaders must admit that the playing field isn't level. Accept the reality that team members are at different places in their career and professional development. The "leader as coach" commits to and invests in the unique development of each team member.

Start where they are. Find out where they want to go. Be their development advocate and provide the time and resources to let them outgrow their current role.

Getting Better Incrementally

The best leaders are lifelong learners who apply behavioral insights into the daily practice of leading. As a result, they continue to refine the habits by which they lead team members, teams, and the entire organization.

Why Leaders Fail in Their Most Essential Competency: Delegation

"I can do it better."

"I can do it faster."

"I don't have time to train anyone to do it."

"Actually, I don't trust my team."

DAY 297

The Delegation ROI

Could you save one hour per week by letting a team member do the portion of your work that they could do and you shouldn't continue to do?

In a year you would recapture more than a full work week of time for more strategic leadership assignments rather than continuing to default to your former tactical or operational expertise.

When You Refuse to Delegate

You become the bottleneck to productivity.

You hinder the development of emerging leaders.

You are working below your paygrade.

You keep yourself busy in operations rather than strategy.

Delegating is a triple win.

You win. Your direct report wins. The organization wins.

The Four Phases of Delegating Responsibility and Authority

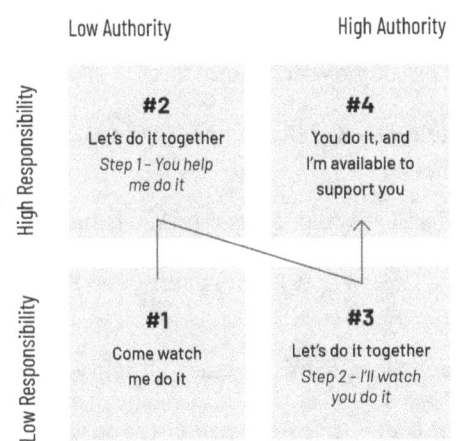

Giving Responsibility and Authority to a Direct Report

Stage One – Low Responsibility and Low Authority

Leader: "Come watch me do this."

Stage Two – High Responsibility and Low Authority

Leader: "Let's do this together. You help me."

Stage Three – Low Responsibility and High Authority

Leader: "Let's do this together. I'll help you."

Stage Four – High Responsibility and High Authority

Leader: "Now it's your responsibility, and I will be available to support you."

Strategic Networking Is Today's Investment in Tomorrow

Identify who you should be connecting with internally and externally to expand your business acumen.

Connections lead to new opportunities.

Connections become a collection of subject matter experts you can turn to when developing your own best practice insights.

How will you connect, and what will be the agenda of your questions?

OCTOBER

DAY 302

When Conflict Divides

Understand the problem.

Separate people from the problem.

Consider scenarios of response.

Find common ground.

Identify a possible solution all can agree to.

Leadership implies stepping into conflict and managing the flow of conflicting ideas in order to find a win-win solution.

DAY 303

The AI World

Staying current with the digital world is not easy. Sharing the learning curve with your team might make it more manageable. Learn together so you can get to a common digital language and shared understanding of the latest developments in AI. Identify what tools are most relevant to add to your leadership effectiveness. Let the rest go … for now.

OCTOBER

Adult Learners

We all learn differently. Some prefer more active learning with hands-on experiences. Others prefer more concept-oriented learning to think through ideas. Leadership development should consider the idea that we all default to a pre-ferred style, but great learning always seeks to internalize new ideas and practice new habits by touching the entire learning cycle.

MONTH 11

NOVEMBER

MONTH

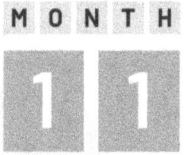

The Pathway of More Effective and Efficient Leadership

Twelve core ideas are reflected in the posts that follow. The assignment for the executive team in any organization is to review the list. Identify the top three and the bottom three. The top three are the commitments already being addressed. The bottom three are the items needing attention. Include a ranking from other employment categories than senior leaders to correct your bias for greater objectivity. Establish three work teams to define and address each of the areas you've neglected. All twelve support the 365 Day Leader who is committed to recalibrate their leadership calling.

NOVEMBER

Twelve Core Ideas

NOVEMBER

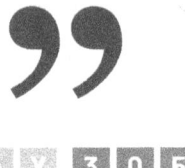

It's Time to Ask #1

Are you a step ahead of your competition? Are you following them, or are they following you? Might you need to swallow pride and collaboratively follow each other?

DAY 306

It's Time to Ask #2

Do you design your best practices through a continual process of incremental tests of change, or do you just accept industry best practices that fit another context but may not be uniquely applicable to your organization?

It's Time to Ask #3

Do you know the limits of your leadership capacity? Do you know how to manage capacity limits? Are you willing to address competency gaps to enhance your leadership capacity?

NOVEMBER

DAY 308

It's Time to Ask #4

Do you know the signs of when a key team member is becoming divisive in undermining your leadership? A common mistake is waiting too long to deal directly with a toxic team member.

NOVEMBER

DAY 309

It's Time to Ask #5

Can you say, "I don't know?"

Can you say, "I'm sorry?"

Can you say, "I was wrong?"

Leading for the long haul requires all three.

It's Time to Ask #6

Do you know the cost of executive rudeness disguised by an attitude of one's importance and busyness? The "nobodys" are always "somebodys" and their perception of you matters in the culture of the company. Stopping throughout the day to connect with people may only take a matter of seconds but it builds a mosaic of respect that positively influences both culture and relationships.

NOVEMBER

It's Time to Ask #7

Do you give credit or prefer to take it? Catch people doing something right more than you catch them making mistakes. Recognize, reward, and celebrate teams and team members. Without them, your work would not get done. When is your next party?

It's Time to Ask #8

Are you breaking through organizational silos by aligning teams to shared outcomes and organizational values with cross-functional strategies spanning across all the typical workplace boundaries?

NOVEMBER

DAY 313

Resilience – Leading for the Long Haul

Every leader will face at least one impossible situation during their leadership tenure. It's when your back is against the wall with no way out, you are completely alone, and you will feel utterly defeated.

Creative staying power increases the odds of making the impossible possible. It will demand every ounce of leadership skill, personal determination, innovative resourcefulness, collaborative effort, emotional intelligence, and physical stamina.

Sustaining leaders will always see an inevitable ending as a new beginning.

Leadership Survival Strategies

Core Values – Find your grounding in the core values that are the beliefs guiding your behavior.

Giving Up – It's the easiest way out, but a mindset sustaining leaders ignore.

One Step – Only focus on the next step that seems apparent and might lead to step two.

Limited Resources – Learn to clarify and classify every possible and atypical resource.

Counterintuitive Thinking – If you are bound by intuitive ideas, it keeps you from getting outside the boundaries of your current limitations.

Access the Experts – Consider your network that offers a mosaic of resources.

DAY 315

Learned Optimism

Leadership challenges distinguish pessimists from optimists.

Pessimists explain life events as if bad things are always bound to happen, and the negative results last forever.

Optimists live with a confident expectation that good things will happen to them in spite of life's difficulties.

Optimistic leaders don't give up.

Optimistic leaders are never the victim.

Optimistic leaders see trouble as a challenge to overcome.

Optimistic leaders bring a resilience that enables them to bounce back after setbacks.

DAY 316

Coaching, Mentoring, Counseling

Coaching An internal or external certified coach who meets with the leader for a specified period of time with focus on one to three leadership competencies or behaviors. Coaching addresses behavioral change to positively affect the perception of the leader by team members.

Mentoring An informal advisory relationship with someone who has greater life experience, work knowledge, or connections and gives advice to someone with less experience, knowledge, or connections.

Counseling Often a retrospective process looking to understand the influence of the past and why it is impacting one's current reality. The counselor is an authority addressing the client's challenges and helping them improve their well-being.

The Development Journey

When a leader has clarity on specific leadership skills that need attention, then the development journey can begin through structured learning translated into new leadership habits.

DAY 318

Developmental Learning

Learning is where leadership development begins, but learning without application is merely an academic exercise with no meaningful return on investment for the business at large.

Organizations Value People

The invitation for organizations committed to growing leaders is to combine their value of development with their investment in that development. In other words, they put their money where their mouth is.

Who Gets Developed?

To develop leaders at every level in the entire organization involves…

Supervisors who provide lower-level oversight of teams

Managers who provide mid-level oversight of teams

Leaders who provide top-level oversight of managers and other leaders

Do You Fit the Organization?

Fit within a team or company is influenced by one's attitudes, motives, values, preferences, background, experience, education, and how closely those align with their organization. When it's not a fit, it will take its toll on the employee, the team, and the organization.

Hiring and Managing

If you do the hard work of hiring well, then the challenging work of managing is easier.

NOVEMBER

DAY 323

The Value of Values

Outstanding values are foundational to an inspiring vision and challenging mission.

NOVEMBER

DAY 324

Challenge, Invest, Develop, and Retain

Where would you place each of your direct reports on this Nine Box Grid?

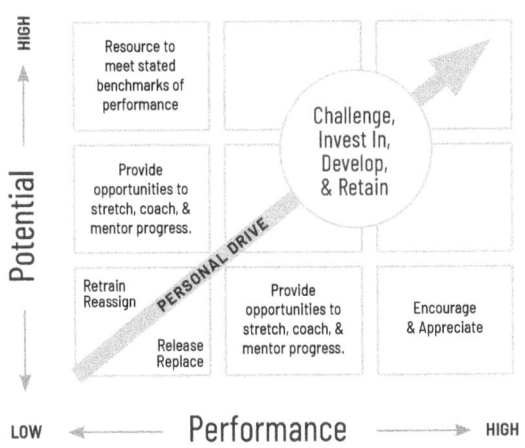

Understanding Each Direct Report

Performance is the degree to which a direct report meets expectations.

Potential is the possibility of direct reports exceeding expectations.

Personal Drive is the reality of one's intensity and intentionality in closing the gap between performance and potential.

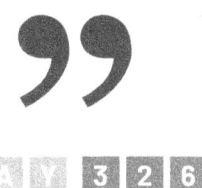

The A Players on Your Team

Your high performers are those with exceptional performance who have the anticipated potential and personal drive to achieve high levels of organizational responsibility.

The Impact of Underperformers

Leveling the playing field always takes the team average down. Underperformers negatively impact everyone else and decrease the productive potential of the entire team.

DAY 328

Enterprise Leadership

Leading at the organizational, system, or enterprise level will require the highest tier of leadership responsibility with a greater emphasis on strategy than on operational tactics. It necessitates a unique mixture of competencies that differ from leading teams or managing individuals.

Culture Assessment Question – Part A

1. Are the vision, mission, values, and strategy clear and consistently communicated?

2. How prevalent are political minefields that must be navigated and negotiated to compete for limited resources?

3. What are the spoken and unspoken rules, and does anyone get a pass?

4. Are there personalities who set the positive or negative mood for everyone else? Do we tolerate the negative, and if so, why?

5. Are there intentional team-building activities that enhance camaraderie and contribute to team trust?

NOVEMBER

DAY 330

Culture Assessment Question – Part B

1. Is the company a collection of silos, or do teams and team members get to work collaboratively across typical workplace boundaries?

2. How is conflict perceived and managed?

3. How is failure addressed and success celebrated?

4. Are people micromanaged or are they given full responsibility and authority to execute their delegated assignments? In other words, how is authority exerted?

5. How is work-life balance modeled and encouraged? How is it handled when an employee is experiencing a great imbalance in this area?

Service Standards Are the Guardrails of Culture

Inclusiveness – Giving every employee the opportunity for professional development.

Clarity – Illustrating the core values and the core competencies needed for success.

Logistics – The practical questions of the pathway to development: Who? Where? When? How?

Modeling – When the C-Suite publicly commits to their own development adventure.

Inspiration – Casting vision to help each individual stretch to their potential.

Celebration – Recognizing each step and each stage of achievement in the development journey.

DAY 332

Leading and Managing

Leaders Mostly Lead

They invest most of their time and attention in strategy (doing the right things) and less in operations (doing things the right way).

Managers Mostly Manage

They invest most of their time in operational tactics (doing things the right way) and less in strategy (doing the right things).

How Do Leaders Invest in Developmental Relationships?

Understand the uniqueness of each direct report.

Be their advocate for growth and development.

Provide the resources for that development.

Challenge them with stretch assignments.

Connect them to new networks that enrich their business acumen.

NOVEMBER

Leading Others

Invest in the individual.

Coach each team member differently.

Ask more than tell.

Initiate career conversations.

Celebrate achievements.

MONTH 12

DECEMBER

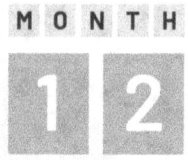

MONTH 12

Stages of Leadership Development

Emerging Leaders

Stage One – Getting Started – *"I have a job"*

Stage Two – Gaining Skills – *"I'm getting better at this"*

Stage Three – Building Knowledge – *"I'm a subject matter expert"*

Developing Leaders

Stage Four – Supervising Others – *"I can manage people"*

Stage Five – Developing People – *"I can lead teams"*

Strategic Leaders

Stage Six – Focusing the Organization – *"I know where we need to go"*

DECEMBER

Manageable and Measurable Stages

Leading Self

In order to lead others, we must first lead ourselves.

1. Leaders who model the way are invested in their own continuing development.
2. They are responsible for their own development. No one will do it for them.
3. They are transparent and vulnerable in asking a colleague or friend where they need to grow further.
3. They only focus on a few manageable growth areas at a time.

DAY 336

A Personal Assessment

The Four-Question Review

1. What am I good at that I should keep doing?
2. What am I good at that I need to get better at because it's so critical to my role?
3. What is the blind spot that gets in the way of my interpersonal effectiveness?
4. What best practices of leading do I need to start doing?

The Leadership Capacity Question: How High Can You Lead?

What's the distance from where you are today to where your potential could take you tomorrow?

How driven are you to get there?

Are you willing to take incremental steps of development?

What area of competence in your current role needs attention first?

A Model of How Development Works

Feedback identifies areas of needed improvement.

Learning informs the development area in focus.

Interaction with a coach or colleague discusses how learning applies.

Application in stretch assignments applies the learning in each iteration of incremental change.

DAY 339

Seven Rules of Self-Reflection

1. Time – When will you stop and reflect?

2. Start small – Incremental is the key idea.

3. Hold yourself accountable – No one will do it for you.

4. Check your feelings – How hard is change?

5. Observe others – Who effectively models the skill you are developing?

6. Ask for feedback – Who knows you are working on this leadership skill?

7. Be forgiving – This is about progress not perfection.

DAY 340

Self-Reflection for Self-Awareness

Self-reflection is a deliberate, honest, and objective review of your thoughts, feelings, emotions, and changes needed in your existing leadership habits.

Feedback from a trusted group of colleagues corrects your personal bias or identifies blind spots to refine your clarity on what to work on next.

Leaders Are Made

The smallest incremental change compounded over time can contribute to the growth and development of core leadership competencies and leadership behaviors.

There are no quick solutions.

Time is your friend.

Take the long-term perspective.

Never quit.

DECEMBER

DAY 342

The Essential Competency Needed by Every Leader

Clear and consistent communication is a must-have skill for every leader.

DECEMBER

DAY 343

How Accountable Are You?

Coaching offers **professional** accountability.

A development culture offers **organizational** accountability.

360-degree feedback offers **team** accountability.

Reflection offers **personal** accountability.

Learning to be More Competent

Coaching helps identify the competencies needing further development.

Micro-learning increases one's understanding in order to apply new ideas.

New skills lead to incremental change in one's habits of leading.

Feedback and reflection guide your next iteration of learning and application and change.

DECEMBER

DAY 345

Green – Yellow – Red: A Culture Tool for Organizational Health

Green – All is well. Let's keep working. Any conflict is between ideas, not individuals. Emotions remain low and are being managed well.

Yellow – We are proceeding with caution. Let's be aware that our competing ideas have an emotional investment in what we are individually advocating.

Red – This meeting is not going well, and we should stop. Conflict is escalating and emotions are becoming more intense. Resentment is possible.

The Team Rule: Teams can agree to call "Green, Yellow, or Red" at any time.

DAY 346

How to Do Personal Reflection

1. Identify and describe each leadership development opportunity you need to address.

2. Explain why it is important for you to work on this area as part of your professional development.

3. Describe the return on investment to your team and your company if you could develop further in this area.

4. Provide a summary of resources you will use for a professional development process.

5. Indicate your means of measurement to validate your progress.

DECEMBER

DAY 347

The Individual Development Plan (IDP)

A plan charts the "what, why, and how" of your work to strengthen your leadership with new sustainable habits. The Plan creates intentionality, focus, accountability, and a timeline.

… What are you working on?

… Why is that important to you?

… How will it benefit the company if you get better in that area?

Day 348

Perfectionists Not Welcome Here

If you're aiming for perfection in your professional development, then don't even start. If you want progress toward your productive potential, then focus on a few manageable leadership skills that are vital to your current and future success.

When leadership development is incremental, then developing new leadership habits is manageable. When it's manageable, then it compounds over time to contribute to the likelihood of sustainability for the long haul.

DAY 349

Is the Value of Professional Development Valuable to You?

If every senior leader does not own and model the value and investment in developing their own leadership skill set, then the identification of new leadership habits for everyone else is hypocritical.

DECEMBER

DAY 350

Are Values Just Good Ideas or Behaviors to Live By?

If organizational values are behaviors and not just ideas to believe, then those behaviors are expected of every employee.

Values as behaviors shape organizational culture and necessitate immediate feedback and consistent accountability for every team member.

DAY 351

Vision and Mission Basics

If the organizational vision and mission do not support the development of every emerging leader, then there is not an inspired goal of what the proposed development work is leading to.

Without clarity of progress toward achieving this identified core outcome, the personal drive to improve and exceed expectations is diminished for even your "high potentials."

DAY 352

The Under and Over Performers

If leaders don't address the under-performer, it levels the playing field down and never up.

If leaders don't include the over-performer in the strategic thinking of how to achieve the vision, then long-term retention of your best team members will be a challenge.

Organizational Lifecycles

Predictable stages of growth or deterioration in the organizational lifecycle provide constructive insight into problems that require change. Every stage includes normal and predictable challenges unique to that stage. Ignore them and it prevents you from the next stage of organizational maturity, organizational health, and organizational potential.

DECEMBER

When Leaders Fail to Delegate

Lack of delegation causes a spiral of missed opportunities to develop and equip employees at all levels of any organization.

The **leader** loses time on more important tasks.

The **team** loses stretch assignments that develop them for more complex assignments.

The **organization** loses out on achieving its productive potential.

The Recognition Variance

Some leaders don't need or want recognition for what they do. Accomplishment is its own reward. The mistake is assuming that everyone on your team is wired the same way. Wrong!

Lack of recognition, reward, and celebration de-motivates some on your team to exceed expectations in existing assignments, let alone to take on more responsibility.

DECEMBER

DAY 356

You Set the Pace for Your Team

Leading yourself is always harder than leading your team. If you fail to lead yourself in professional development, then don't expect your team to do it either. Few will ever go further or faster than their leader, so lead the way!

DECEMBER

DAY 357

Vulnerability and Transparency

Be open about your best and worst. Listen to the perceptions others have of you from a select group of work associates. It requires a maturity that doesn't over interpret or under interpret the good, bad, or ugly about yourself. Then get to work on growing further as a leader.

As We Grow, We Change

The Gallup research behind the Clifton StrengthsFinder Assessment is a reminder that we don't change but rather become more of who we already are. We can improve but not become someone different. So don't try to be someone else. Keep becoming the best that you can be!

DECEMBER

What Are You Rewarded For?

We too easily perform according to what is rewarded. In our increasingly busy world, the urgent outpaces the important. As a result, we ignore our professional development and rationalize procrastination once again. Our "one-day" dream never seems to come, and we settle for something less than our potential. It is a short-sighted perspective by organizations who allow procrastination to continue indefinitely because their "urgent" replaces your "important."

DAY 360

The Sequence of Getting Better

Learning leads to application, and application leads to new habitual ways of leading.
It is the moment in organizational life when leadership development touches performance, engagement, satisfaction, attraction, retention, and productivity all at once.

DECEMBER

DAY 361

How Blind Are You?

Who will you ask to give you honest feedback about your blind spots? When?

DECEMBER

DAY 362

Too Arrogant or Too Humble?

What is one thing you could do differently to avoid arrogance and practice genuine humility?

DECEMBER

Your Retirement Party

Do you want people to recall your accomplishments or recognize and respect your values?

Do people know your values?

Do people see your values?

Do you lead in such a way that people know and see what you value most?

DAY 364

An Aligned Organization

When was the last time you reviewed and evaluated the alignment among your vision, mission, values, strategy, structure, staffing, and systems?

The list is dynamic, but it is also linear and sequential. Each word is directly impacted by the previous word starting with your vision and ending with the systems.

Systems support staffing. Staffing supports structure. Structure supports strategy. Strategy supports values. Values support mission. Mission supports vision.

Feeling Guilty

Do you ever feel guilty using work time for your own professional development as if you are cheating the organization or somehow not doing your job?

Worse yet, do you make your team feel guilty when they take time for professional development?

Remember, increasing competence adds value to the organization and enhances your indispensability to the organization.

This is how you keep bringing your best self to your best work.

AFTERWORD

THE SUM OF IT ALL

RECALIBRATING YOUR CALLING EVERY DAY

THE 365 DAY LEADER DEBRIEF

You don't need to win every battle. Your real "war" is what is needed to live out your daily mission on the way to achieving your vision.

If every critic, constructive or toxic, puts you on the defensive, then there is not only something wrong with them but with you too. Understand the people and situations that trigger the worst in you. Learn the EQ techniques to manage the valid emotions you are feeling. Seven steps of how to begin in the moment of confrontation:

1. Thank them for their feedback. (You've just diffused their motive and your reaction.)

2. Tell them you will give their idea some thought. (You've just taken control of the potentially defensive moment.)

3. Ask a few trusted colleagues or friends if their comment has any credibility. (Now you are broadening the circle of conversation for greater objectivity.)

4. If it's serious enough to necessitate a meeting, never go alone. Bring a neutral third party to moderate and know what was said and how it was said. (This protects you from the "he said, she said" dynamic when no one ever knows for sure what really happened.)

5. Get back to the person with your reply in light of the feedback from others. (This step enables you to distinguish between their personal preference and your leadership principle in light of how others have responded to their proposal. It's often true that there is more than one way to do anything. Their idea isn't necessarily right, and yours isn't necessarily wrong. Your idea isn't necessarily the only way to do this, and their idea may not be totally wrong. If there is something to learn from their suggestion, then compromise in a win-win solution. If it is merely their preference versus your principle, then be ready with the rationale of your approach reinforced by the objective feedback from the individuals you spoke with.)

6. Thank them once again and invite them to be part of winning the war with you rather than fighting a battle against you. (Now you have offered them a choice. Let them choose while you move on to the bigger war ... unoffended.)

7. The calling of leadership is to be trusted and respected not liked. (The people who like you will show up at your retirement party and celebrate their trust and respect of who you are and the wars you've won.)

Learning and Leading with You,

Dr. D

DICK DANIELS

www.theLDG.org

ACKNOWLEDGEMENTS

Noteworthy writing is always a collaborative process. An inspired idea launches the author into the journey of their best attempt at wordsmithing the original vision. Personal review, peer feedback, professional editing, and creative design are essential non-negotiables to take a good idea and make it even better. I am grateful for a gracious and capable team.

MARSHALL GOLDSMITH has offered the endorsement quote on the last three of my writing projects. His bestselling library is evidence of the recognition from voices across the leadership development and coaching enterprise. My Master Coach certification comes from Marshall's Stakeholder Centered Coaching methodology. His team includes current thought leaders in this genre of leadership literature. He inspires the best out of authors and coaches, and he freely gives away all of his intellectual capital as a contribution to others who will listen. *https://mgscc.net*

JOHN PEARSON has been a peer and professional colleague since our grad school days in Chicago. He has led the way nationally and globally advising non-profits on board policy governance. His insight into the relevant applications of the John Carver model brings clarity to the leadership of the board and the leadership of the staff. His Weekly Staff Meeting email spotlights the best and the brightest of organizational and leadership development in his insightful and thorough book reviews. *https://www.johnpearsonassociates.com*

HEIDI SHEARD is a freelance editor with whom I have worked on all four leadership books from The Leadership Development Group. She is exceptionally skilled in creating a consistent voice throughout each project. In these last nine years, she has discovered how I think and write. In each book, she enhances the writing quality in terms of clarity and brevity. Heidi shares in all the success of the awards received for each writing initiative.

KENDAL MARSH is Principal at the Brand Office. Kendal's team brings shared expertise to all aspects of book design. It starts with the front cover, moves to the back cover and continues with creativity on each page throughout the entire book. In each project, he brings conceptual ideas for review and discussion. The final copy always surprises me in the professionalism and visual appeal that connects to the title and theme of the entire book with intentionality and continuity.

ABOUT THE AUTHOR

DR. DICK DANIELS is a Certified Leadership Development Master Coach with twenty years of executive development expertise across all industry sectors. He excels in identifying unique leadership growth areas for individual development planning and enhanced leadership performance.

- A thought leader in organizational development with 125 + clients in six- to eighteen-month coaching engagements.

- Daniels is the Founder and President of The Leadership Development Group and hosts the LinkedIn group by that same name where more than 200,000 global leadership practitioners collaborate in ongoing conversations about leadership development best practices.

- Daniels has written three nationally awarded leadership books: *Leadership Briefs*, *Leadership Core*, and *Hardwiring New Leadership Habits*.

- He has also written three awarded children's books in the *Oak Street Treehouse* trilogy.

- He is a board member for Hodos Institute, which provides ethical and effective leadership research and training in Ukraine.

His passion is walking alongside leaders at every level in any organization to contribute to their effectiveness and efficiency with a healthy work-life balance. His legacy is three amazing adult children and seven awesome grandchildren who remind him daily just how blessed he really is.

The 365 Day Leader Topic Reference Guide

TOPIC	DAY
Accountability	51, 84, 141, 231, 267, 292, 294, 343
Adult Learning	304
AI	303
Arrogance	67, 200, 362
Bias	18, 125
Blind Spots	244, 361
Capacity	10, 11, 14, 23, 189, 190
Change	201, 202, 205, 227, 275, 358
Character	2, 4, 10, 117, 118, 138
Coaching	3, 122, 161, 237, 294, 316, 320, 333, 342
Collaboration	218, 220
Communication	165, 175, 178, 234, 235, 238, 279
Competence	2, 9, 10, 65
Conflict	219, 302, 345
Crisis and Stress	285
C-Suite	253, 263
Cultural Fit	254, 321
Culture	13, 43, 64, 86, 121, 155, 171, 180, 186, 242, 262, 329, 330, 331
Decisions	153
Delegation	27, 191, 296, 297, 298, 299, 300, 354

TOPIC	DAY

Development 34, 37, 39, 56, 57, 106, 172, 190, 193, 194, 215, 226, 230, 243, 281, 283, 317, 318, 338

Development Model 338

Direct Reports 50, 177, 188, 221, 225, 325, 326, 333

Emotions 59, 137, 197, 198, 199, 245

Empathy 80, 150, 255

End and Means 22

Engagement 233, 256

Ethics 7, 17, 58, 66, 258, 259

Execution 214

Failure 144, 164, 170, 248, 249, 250, 260, 265, 291

Feedback 86

Followership 38

Gratitude 29, 103, 139, 264

Habits of Leadership 40, 69-79, 128-132

Hard Skills/Soft Skills 210

Head and Heart 80

Heart and Head 80

Hiring 30, 135, 216, 280, 322

Humility 246-247

Humor 162, 257

Incremental Change 295, 341, 344

Integrity 19

TOPIC	DAY
Leader	15, 18, 24, 28, 33, 38, 42, 47, 53, 55, 82, 229, 278, 290, 334, 335
Leadership	38, 83, 102, 105, 107, 108, 123, 124, 127, 134, 136, 163, 187, 207, 208, 266, 268
Leading Self	336, 337, 339, 340, 349, 357, 360, 363, 365
Learning	31
Listening	147
Management	90-101, 152, 332
Means and End	22
Meetings	41, 146, 156, 223, 224, 284
Micromanaging	269, 282
Mission and Vision	49, 87, 88, 183, 185, 351
Mistakes	144, 164, 170, 248, 249, 250, 260, 265, 291
Model	166, 356
Networking	45, 301
Nine Box Grid	133, 324
Non-Verbals	81, 270
Onboarding	86
Organization	1, 8, 16, 21, 24, 38, 192, 269, 319, 328, 353, 364
Organizational Politics	151
Peers	252
Perception	120, 140, 251, 287, 289
Perfectionist	271, 348
Personal Drive	6

TOPIC	DAY
Priorities	212, 213
Process Improvement	276
Procrastination	154, 272
Productive Potential	38
Promotion	286
Productivity	12, 126, 142
Professional and/or Personal	222
Professional Development Plan	347
Questions	20, 54, 60-63, 68, 104, 109-116, 148, 179, 236, 288, 305-312, 329-330, 336, 337
Recognition	240, 355, 359
Reflection	35, 274, 268, 269, 339, 340, 346
Resilience	313, 314, 315
Strategy	145, 149, 157, 158, 160, 167, 169, 174, 203, 204, 206, 209, 228, 273, 277, 293
Succession Planning	5, 239
Sympathy	80
Teams	24, 32, 44, 46, 48, 119, 159, 168, 173, 176
Time	89, 143, 211
Toxic Personality	36, 217, 241, 261
Trust	181, 182, 196
Underperformer	52, 232, 327, 352
Urgent/Important	85
Values	25, 26, 184, 195, 242, 323, 350

Lead Unoffended

Every supervisor, manager, or leader will be the bull's eye on someone's target. They may not be like you. They may not like you. They may assume you took the job that was rightfully theirs. Regardless of their reason or motive, the offenders are always out there somewhere ... someday. It's not "if." It's "when."

If leaders don't have the emotional resilience to withstand those subtle or blatant attacks ... or attacks camouflaged in someone's attempt at humor, then don't lead. Be an individual contributor or a team member on another leader's work team. The question for anyone contemplating a leadership role is: **Can you lead unoffended?**

www.ingramcontent.com/pod-product-compliance
Lightning Source LLC
LaVergne TN
LVHW022233080526
838199LV00120B/598/J